D1983767

International Business English

Communication skills in English for business purposes

Workbook

Leo Jones
Richard Alexander

Ernst Klett Verlag
Cambridge University Press

Published by the Press Syndicate of the University of Cambridge
The Pitt Building, Trumpington Street, Cambridge CB2 1RP
40 West 20th Street, New York, NY 10011, USA
10 Stamford Road, Oakleigh, Melbourne 3166, Australia

© Cambridge University Press 1989

First published 1989

Printed in Great Britain
at the University Press, Cambridge

Werkübersicht
ISBN 3–12–502770–5 Workbook
ISBN 3–12–502750–0 Student's Book
ISBN 3–12–502760–8 Teacher's Book
ISBN 3–12–502790–X Set of 2 self-study cassettes
ISBN 3–12–502780–2 Set of 3 class cassettes

Beratende Mitwirkung an diesem Werk:

Peter Kirchhoff, Fachbereichsleiter Fremdsprachen an der Volkschochschule Wuppertal, Landesprüfungsbeauftragter für das Volkshochschul-Zertifikat English for Business Purposes in Nordrhein-Westfalen

ISBN 3-12-502770-5

1. Auflage 1 4 3 2 1 | 1992 91 90 89

Alle Drucke dieser Auflage können im Unterricht nebeneinander benutzt werden, sie sind untereinander unverändert. Die letzte Zahl bezeichnet das Jahr dieses Druckes.
© dieser Ausgabe: Ernst Klett Verlage GmbH u. Co. KG, Stuttgart 1989.
Alle Rechte vorbehalten.

Contents

Vorwort

International Business English ist ein Lehrwerk für Lernende, die im Wirtschaftsleben tätig sind und Englisch im Beruf verwenden müssen. Ebenso eignet es sich für erwachsene Lernende, die am Ende ihrer Ausbildung in Wirtschaft und Handel tätig sein werden.

Der Begriff *Business English*

- Obgleich man einen bestimmten Teil des englischen Wortschatzes als *Business*- oder Wirtschaftsvokabular bezeichnen kann, ist dennoch ein großer Teil dessen, was man als Wirtschaftsenglisch bezeichnet, nichts weiter als 'normales' Englisch, das in wirtschaftlichen Zusammenhängen angewendet wird. Wirtschaftsenglisch ist also keine Spezialsprache. Das Lehrwerk bietet eine Fülle von Geschäftsanlässen und Situationen als Grundlage für gezielte Übung. Sie erweitern Ihre Englischkenntnisse, gewinnen mehr Selbstvertrauen und können sich letztlich flüssiger und präziser ausdrücken.

Das *Workbook* und die *Workbook-Cassetten*

Das *Workbook* und die *Workbook-Cassetten* enthalten

- ergänzendes Material zum Üben von Grammatik und Sprechfunktionen.
- ergänzendes Übungsmaterial für lautes Lesen (mit Musterpassagen auf der Cassette zum Vergleich).
- ergänzendes Übungsmaterial zum Grundwortschatz in Wirtschaftsenglisch.
- zusätzliches Übungsmaterial zu den Präpositionen und zur Wortbildung.
- zusätzliche Aufgabenstellungen zum Abfassen von Briefen, Fernschreiben und Berichten.
- zusätzliche Hörverständnisaufgaben auf den Cassetten.
- einen Lösungsschlüssel zu allen Übungen.

Abschließend noch ein Hinweis für die Arbeit mit dem *Workbook*. Grundsätzlich sollten Sie immer auf Ihr persönliches Wissen und Ihre Berufserfahrung zurückgreifen. Ihr Sprachlehrer wird Ihnen zwar helfen, Ihre Sprachkenntnisse zu verbessern. Der Wirtschaftsexperte jedoch sind Sie letztlich selbst.
Wir wünschen Ihnen viel Freude beim Englischlernen mit *International Business English*!

Introduction

What does the Workbook contain?

There are several kinds of exercises in this Workbook:

Vocabulary – revision of vocabulary presented in the activities and texts in the Student's Book
Grammar – extra practice in using the structures presented in the Student's Book
Prepositions (in units 5 to 15) – using prepositions and prepositional phrases
Word-building (in units 5, 7, 9, 11, 13 and 15) – using prefixes and suffixes to form words
Reading aloud – extra practice following up the Student's Book exercises
Functions – extra practice in using the expressions presented in the Student's Book (some of these are recorded exercises on the self-study cassettes)
Listening – listening to and understanding interviews, broadcasts and discussions on business topics; there are also note-taking tasks based on recorded messages on the self-study cassettes
Writing – short writing tasks with model versions in the Answer Key

and at the back of the book:
The Answer Key – with answers to all the exercises

What is on the self-study cassettes?

The two self-study cassettes contain listening exercises and speaking exercises. Full instructions on what to do are given in the Workbook itself.

The listening exercises usually consist of several tasks and you'll need to listen to the recording more than once. If your cassette player has a counter, make sure you set it to zero at the start of each exercise, so that you can easily find the beginning again. In the speaking exercises you'll need to 'talk to the tape', but there's usually no need to record your own voice. If you do want to record your own voice, you'll need to use a blank cassette of your own. The speaking exercises give further practice in using the functional expressions and in reading aloud. They will help you to develop your fluency.

How do I use the Workbook and the Answer Key?

The Vocabulary, Grammar, Functions, Reading Aloud and Writing exercises contain follow-up work on language points that are presented in the equivalent sections of the Student's Book. You'll usually find it easier to do these Workbook exercises after you've done the equivalent sections in the Student's Book.

The Prepositions, Word-building, Listening and Reading exercises are related to the theme of the Student's Book unit, but not directly to any particular section in the unit.

The **Answer Key** contains answers to all the exercises. It is there so that you can check your own answers. For some exercises, the answers we give are 'suggested answers': this means that variations are often possible which are equally correct. If you don't understand **why** some of your answers are wrong or different from the model answers given, you may need to ask your teacher about this.

If possible, try to refer to the Answer Key **after** you've tried each exercise. You'll find that you'll learn better by looking at the answers later and that the exercises are more enjoyable if you have to think hard about them.

With the Writing tasks, once you have compared your work with the model version in the Key, you may need to ask your teacher to look at your work and show you where you have made any mistakes in grammar, spelling or punctuation.

Should I do all the exercises in the Workbook?

As your time is probably limited and certainly precious, you'll need to **select** which exercises to do in the Workbook. You should decide which of the exercises will be most useful and interesting for you, bearing in mind what you have done in class for each unit. If necessary, ask your teacher for advice.

As a general rule, if you've found a particular language point easy in class, don't do the equivalent exercise in the Workbook. If you find a particular skill difficult, you should spend time on developing this skill using the Workbook exercises – for example if you find it hard to understand people talking English at a natural speed, you should spend plenty of time doing the listening exercises using the self-study cassettes.

What else can I do on my own?

Reading, listening and speaking: As well as working through this Workbook, you should try to seek opportunities of reading, listening to and speaking English in other ways. It may be worth subscribing to a weekly newspaper, such as The Economist. It may be a good idea to listen to radio programmes in English, such as the BBC World Service, or going to the cinema or watching videos to see films in the original English version. And, of course, it will certainly be valuable to take any opportunities to speak English to people – visitors to your company or language institute, tourists, friends of friends, etc.

Preparation: You can save time in class by preparing the sections you will be doing in class – read them through and look up any unfamiliar words.

After class: You can help yourself to remember by reading through the sections you did in class again. This can be done quickly and will be a great help in memorizing new vocabulary and expressions.

Vocabulary – Use a pocket-size notebook to write down new, useful vocabulary and expressions. Writing things down is another way of helping yourself to memorize them and an easy way of looking them up later when you need to refresh your memory. If you come across an unfamiliar word (like *precious* in the first line of the previous section), you should look it up in an English to English dictionary and – if you think it will be useful in future – write it down in your vocabulary book.

We recommend that you invest in an English–English learner's dictionary – ask your teacher to suggest a good one.

Good luck!

1 Face to face

1.1 Asking questions *Grammar*

Before you do these exercises, look at 1.2 in the Student's Book.

A Imagine that you're talking to someone who talks rather unclearly, and that you can't catch some of the information he gives you.
Write down the questions you'd ask this person to find out the missing (~~~) information. The first two are done for you as examples.

1. 'I work for ~~~.'
   Who do you work for ?
2. 'I live in ~~~.'
   Where do you live ?
3. 'I've been working here for ~~~ years.'
   How .... ?
4. 'We keep our sales files in the ~~~ room.'
   Which .... ?
5. 'We never phone in the morning because ~~~.'
   Why .... ?
6. 'I started working for this firm in 19~~.'
   When .... ?
7. 'I'd like a ~~ room for two nights, please.'
   What kind of .... ?
8. 'I heard about this product from Mr ~~~.'
   Who .... ?
9. 'The complete package costs only $~~'
   How much .... ?
10. 'They printed ~~ thousand copies of the company report.'
    How many .... ?

B In these sentences the 'question tags' are missing. Complete each sentence with a suitable tag. The first two are done for you as examples.

1. They don't normally pay their account late, do they.........?
2. The phone number is 518361, isn't it...........?
3. They'll let us know before the end of the month, ...?
4. We can send the catalogues by surface mail, ...?
5. They can't provide us with the information we need, ...?
6. She isn't in the office today, ...?
7. This machine doesn't operate automatically, ...?
8. You know a great deal about economics, ...?
9. You've studied this subject for some time, ...?
10. We shouldn't interrupt the meeting, ...?

C Now rewrite the sentences in exercise B, using the alternative expressions given below. The first two are done for you as examples.

1. I don't think they normally pay their account late. ....
2. I think their phone number is 518361. Is that right? ....
3. .... that's right, isn't it?
4. Am I right in saying that ....?
5. I don't think that ....
6. Is it true that ....?
7. As far as I know, ...
8. I think ....
9. I expect ....
10. I don't think ....

You'll find correct answers to these three exercises in the Answer Key.

1.2 Have you met...? *Functions*

Before you do these exercises, look at 1.4 in the Student's Book.

A WELCOME TO MERIDIAN INTERNATIONAL!

You're going to play the role of CHRIS STEINER. Imagine that you've just joined Meridian International and you'll be introduced to various people in the firm. Reply to each person when you hear the «beep» sound.

Look at these examples and listen to the recording: what you have to say is printed in **bold type**.

Ted: Well, Jean, I'd just like you to meet Chris Steiner. Chris, this is Jean Leroi, he's our Export Manager.

Mr Leroi: How do you do.

«beep»

You: **How do you do, Mr Leroi.**

Mr Leroi: Nice to meet you, Chris. How are you?

«beep»

You: **I'm fine thanks. It's nice to meet you too.**

You may need to PAUSE THE TAPE to give yourself enough time to think before you speak.

B WHAT WOULD YOU SAY?

What would you say in these situations? Write down the exact words you'd use. The first is done for you as an example.

1. The customer services manager, Mrs Hanson, doesn't know Linda Morris, the new export clerk.
   'Mrs Hanson, I'd like you to meet Linda Morris. She's our new export clerk.' ....
2. Your boss says to you, 'This is Tony Watson. He's visiting us from Canada.'
3. Tony Watson says, 'Hi. I think you know one of my colleagues: Ann Scott.'
4. You've been introduced to someone by name, but later in the conversation you can't remember the person's name.
5. You enter an office full of strangers one morning. Someone asks if they can help you.
6. A visitor arrives after travelling a long distance to see you.
7. Your visitor looks thirsty.
8. It's time for you to leave. You look at your watch and see that it's later than you thought.

1.3 Around the world *Vocabulary*

Look at section 1.5 in the Student's Book before you do this exercise.

A Complete each sentence with the appropriate nationality word. Then add the words to the puzzle below. Remember to use Capital Letters. The first one is done for you as an example.

1. If he comes from Cairo, he must be ..Egyptian.............. .
2. If she lives in Paris, she must be ....
3. If they live in Brussels, my guess is that they're ....
4. If they live in São Paulo, they're probably ....
5. If she comes from Geneva, she's ...., I suppose.
6. He works in Vienna, so I think he's ....
7. As she's from Copenhagen, I presume she's ....
8. If he comes from Toronto, he probably speaks ....
9. If she lives in Sofia, she may well be ....
10. As they live in Athens, I think they're ....

11. He lives in Rome, so I suppose he's ....
12. Her home town is Amsterdam, so I guess she's ....
13. Their head office is in Stockholm: they are a .... firm.
14. If they work in Lisbon, I expect they're ....
15. He has a house in Istanbul, so he must be ....

16. If they come from Edinburgh and Cardiff, they're both ....

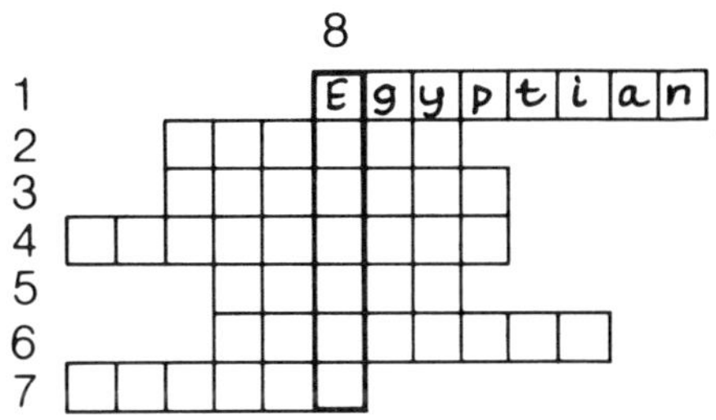

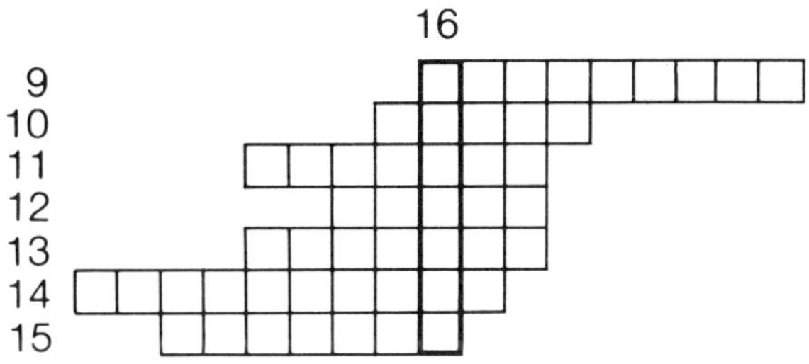

B Name the countries shown in black on this map of the world and write the names in the spaces in the puzzle below. The first is done for you, as an example.
The initial letters of these countries spell two Asian countries where English is widely used for business purposes.

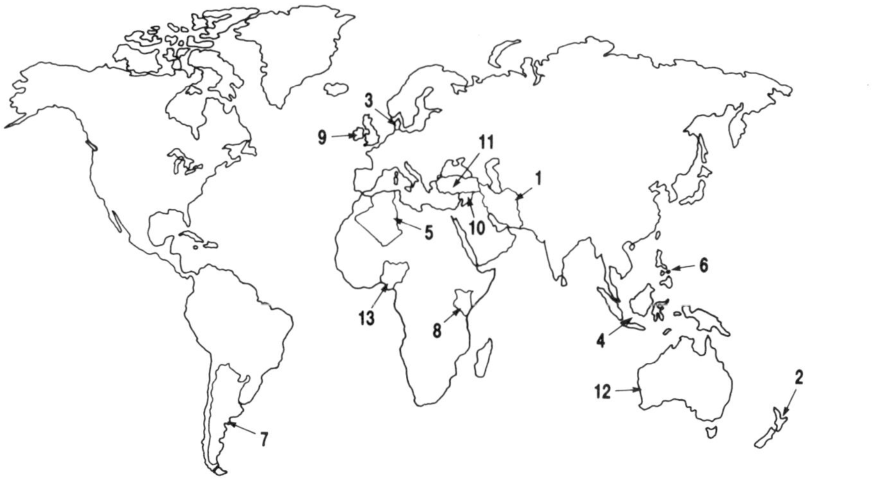

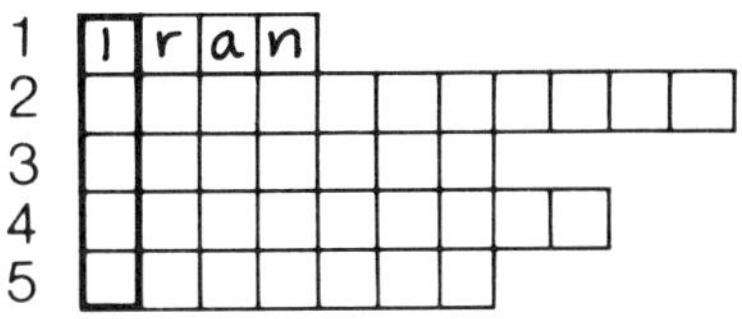

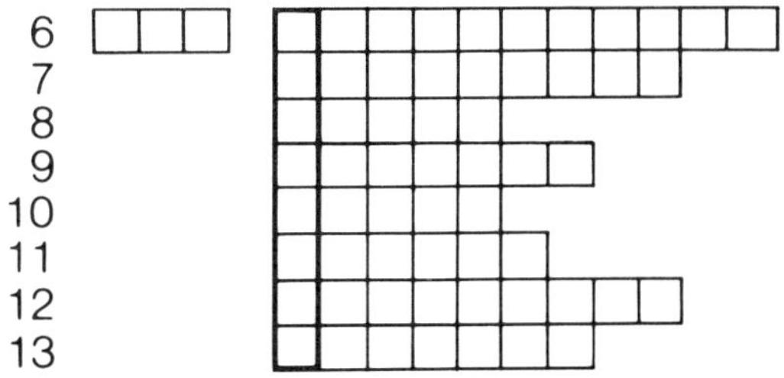

2 Letters, telexes and memos

2.1 Spelling and punctuation mistakes

Look at these two extracts from correspondence, which both contain errors. The first is a part of a letter containing 13 spelling mistakes, the second is part of a telex that contains 13 punctuation mistakes. Find the mistakes and correct them.

Dear Madame,
Thank you very much for your letter and the inclosed literature, wich we recieved on Thurday 7 July. The infomation it contained was quiet interesting and we would like futher details on several produkts in the cataloge:

No.	44/77	Is this availaible in White?
No.	78/612	What is the diskount price of this for orders of over 500 peices?
No.	34/009	Is this compatable with your 55/88 device?

I AM AFRAID, THAT WE HAVE NOT BEEN ABLE TO CONTACT YOU BY TELEPHONE   MY SECRETARY CALLED THROUGHOUT THE DAY YESTERDAY AT HALF-HOURLY INTERVAL'S BUT WAS TOLD THAT YOU WERE NOT AVAILABLE"; PLEASE CONTACT ME PERSONALLY AS SOON AS POSSIBLE. BECAUSE WE NEED TO CHECK A NUMBER OF DETAIL'S IN YOUR ORDER? YOU CAN REACH ME BY TELEPHONE AT ANY TIME THIS AFTERNOON OR TOMORROW MORNING. OUR OFFICE HOURS' ARE 8.30 TO 5 YOU CAN LEAVE A MESSAGE FOR ME, TO CALL YOU BACK IF NECESSARY

2.2 Take a letter . . .

Vocabulary

Fill the gaps in these sentences and write the missing words in the spaces in the puzzle below.

1. A ...clear..... layout is important in a letter.
2. I .... a cheque for £19.99.
3. Esq. is short for ....
4. Your ref. is short for Your ....
5. Remember to put the .... on a letter to the USA.
6. Remember to put the .... on a letter to the UK.
7. If you sign a letter on someone else's behalf, add .... before the other person's name.
8. We .... receipt of your letter.
9. Some documents are printed in two ....
10. Typewriters are being replaced by ....
11. Readers tend to notice the .... of a letter.
12. Memo is short for ....
13. Products are described in a .... (US).
14. Products are described in a .... (GB).
15. This unit is all about ....

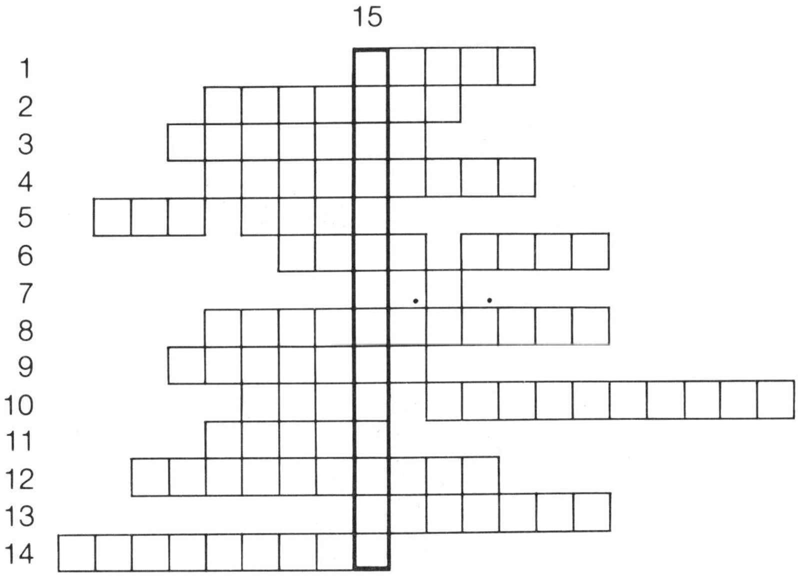

2.3 Should we send them a fax or a telex? *Listening*

01 WHAT IS A FACSIMILE?

☐ A facsimile is an accurate reproduction, probably of a written or typed document, a drawing or a photograph.

02 WHAT IS A FAX MACHINE?

☐ A fax machine copies documents electronically and then transmits them by telephone to a second fax machine which prints out the fascimile. In other words, imagine two photocopiers linked by a telephone line. One may be in London, the other in Luton, Limerick or Lagos. Put the original document into one and on command, an exact replica emerges from the other.

03 WHY A FAX AND NOT A TELEX?

☐ Telex can send and receive only printed text according to a prescribed format. A fax machine sends and receives an exact copy of any image – typescript, handwriting, drawings or photographs.

A Before you listen to the recording, read the questions below. From your own knowledge of the subject, note down *your* answers to the questions:

04 **HOW MUCH DO THEY COST?**
05 **WHAT DOES IT COST TO LEASE A FAX MACHINE?**
06 **ARE FACSIMILES AS GOOD AS THE ORIGINALS?**
07 **CAN I BE SURE THAT THE FACSIMILE IS CORRECT?**
08 **WHAT DOES IT COST TO SEND A FAX?**
09 **CAN I TAKE ADVANTAGE OF CHEAP RATES?**
10 **HOW DO I KNOW IF MY MESSAGE HAS GOT THROUGH?**
11 **HOW CAN I KEEP TRACK OF MY FAX TRAFFIC?**
12 **DOES A FAX TAKE UP MUCH SPACE?**
13 **ARE THEY NOISY?**
14 **DOES A FAX NEED A TRAINED OPERATOR?**
15 **IS A FACSIMILE A LEGAL DOCUMENT?**

B Listen to Beth Simmonds talking to her department head, Mr Newman, about fax machines. Note down the information she gives in answer to questions 04 to 15 above.

C Compare your notes with the answers in the key.

2.4 Make a good impression

We think you'll agree that this letter doesn't make a very good impression on the reader.

1. Decide what can be improved.
2. Rewrite the letter in your own words.
3. Compare your version with the letter in the key.

Dear Mr Brown,

What an unexpected pleasure to hear from you after all this time! We thought you must have forgotten us since you placed your previous order with us two years ago.

May I take this opportunity of enclosing for your attention our new catalogue and price lists. One of the things you'll probably notice is that all the prices have gone up by 15% since your last order but still, never mind, everyone else's have gone up too – even yours I expect! Nevertheless, for your current order, we shall be delighted to supply you at the old price, so you're quite lucky.

Oh, and another thing, I nearly forgot: we've now got a fax machine, so you can contact us by fax if you feel like it. The number is 998321, all right?

So, there we are, nice to be writing to you again.

Yours faithfully,

A. Burke

Sales Director

2.5 Can you tell me how to spell that?

Look at the pairs of words on the next page: one of each is spelt wrongly, the other correctly.

A Decide which spellings are correct and cross out the incorrect ones.

B Play the recording but PAUSE the tape after each number and spell the correct word out loud, like this:

Voice on tape: 'One.'
You: – *PAUSE the tape, then speak:*
'A.C.K.N.O.W.L.E.D.G.E.'
– *Then release PAUSE*
Voice on tape: 'Acknowledge: A.C.K.N.O.W.L.E.D.G.E.'

1. acknowlege acknowledge
2. accommodation acommodation
3. aquire acquire
4. across accross
5. adress address
6. altogether alltogether
7. approximatively approximately
8. independent independant
9. insentive incentive
10. itinerary itinerery
11. misselaneous miscellaneous
12. office stationery office stationary
13. permanant permanent
14. preferential preferentiel
15. pronounciation pronunciation
16. received recieved
17. reccomend recommend
18. recipient recipiant
19. seperate separate
20. simultaneous simultaneus

2.6 Joining sentences *Grammar*

Before you do these exercises, look at 2.5 in the Student's Book.

A In these sentences '*and*' is used with different meanings. Rewrite each sentence, beginning with the words below. The first is done for you as an example.

1. First we will check our inventory *and* then let you know our delivery date.
   After we have checked our inventory, we will let you know our delivery date.
2. Please send us another copy of your invoice *and* we will pay it at once.
   If ………………………………………… .
3. The consignment was packed for export *and* loaded on to the truck.
   Before ………………………………………… .
4. Each order is manufactured *and* the packaging is printed at the same time.
   While ………………………………………… .

5. Your letter was delayed in the post *and* we have not been able to process your order yet.
   Because ....

6. Please inform us of your telex number *and* we will be able to reply to your query at once.
   So that ....

Compare your sentences with the ones in the Answer Key before you begin section B.

B Now complete these sentences in the same way. Again, the first is done for you as an example.

1. The reason why he applied for a job abroad was to earn more money.
   So that he could earn more money, he applied for a job abroad.
2. A single man couldn't lift the package because it was very heavy.
   The package was so ....
3. The order arrived late but we were able to supply the goods on time.
   Although ....
4. There was fog at the airport, but our plane landed safely.
   In spite of ....
5. As there was a mistake in the hotel booking, I had to find another hotel.
   Because of ....
6. The reason why I sent a telex was that I wanted to avoid any mistakes.
   In order to ....

Compare your sentences with the ones in the Answer Key before you begin section C.

C Here are some paragraphs with very short sentences. Join some of the sentences together to make one or two longer sentences, using *and* and other conjunctions or adverbial phrases. The first is done for you as an example.

1. There was a technical problem. The assembly line stopped. The workers were sent home early.
   The workers were sent home early when the assembly line stopped due to a technical problem.
2. Your letter to us was posted yesterday. Our letter to you was posted yesterday. The letters crossed in the post.
3. Our company has a long tradition. Our letters look old-fashioned. We are trying to modernize the company's image. All our correspondence should be word-processed.
4. Short sentences are easy to write. Short sentences are easy to understand. Long words can be confusing. A simple style of writing letters is recommended.

2.7 Improve these letters

Here are three extracts from letters that break some rules.

1. Decide what is wrong with each one and underline any mistakes or faults.
2. Rewrite each extract in your own words.

A

I noticed your advertisment in the Daily Planet amd I would be gratefull if you could sned me further information about your products My company is considering subcontracting some of its office services and I believe that you may be able ot supply us with a sutiable service, Looking forware to hearing form you. Yours faithfully.

B

Thank you very much for you letter of 15 January, which we received today. I answer to your enquiry we have pleasure in enclosing an information pack, giving full details of our services. If you would like any further information, do please contact me by phone or in writing and I will be pleased to help. I hope that our services will be of interest to you and I look forward to hearing from you. Yours sincerely,

C

There are a number of queries that I would like to raise about your products and I would be grateful if you could ask a representative to get in touch with me with a view to discussing these queries and hopefully placing an order if the queries are satisfactorily answered.

3 On the phone

3.1 Misunderstandings on the phone

Listening

On the phone, it's easy to be misunderstood. In part one you'll have to try to understand some people talking quickly and unclearly. In part two you'll hear some advice on how to avoid misunderstandings.

PART ONE

Which of this information is given as these orders are placed over the phone?

300 kilos of white mice	300 kilos of white rice
18 cents per kilo	80 cents per kilo
2 boxes striped pyjamas	2 boxes ripe bananas
£115 per case	£150 per case
So the total price is 4,295 francs.	So the total price is 4,259 francs.
Our phone number is 456892.	Our phone number is 456982.

Check your answers in the key before you begin part two.

PART TWO

You'll hear part of a talk in which a training officer is giving advice to a group of trainees on telephone technique. Listen to the recording and fill the gaps in the summary below:

1. State your name and your .... in the company slowly and clearly.
2. Make sure you're talking to the ....
3. Say right away what you're calling about, the other person shouldn't have to .... this or work it out.
4. Be ...., remember that the other person may have other things to do than talk to you on the phone.
5. If it's a ...., say that you'll .... at once. Then start the call again.
6. Speak slowly and clearly. But in a .... voice.
7. .... while you're speaking. Don't let the other person misunderstand your attitude as being unfriendly.
8. Don't use .... terms or ...., because the other person may not understand as well as you do.
9. Give important information, like ...., ..., ..., dates and so on, slowly and carefully.
10. Make sure the other person has noted the important information down correctly – especially ....
11. Don't .... him or her even if you think you know what he wants to say.
12. If possible, don't phone during the other person's .... or just before he's about to stop work for the day – find out what time it is in the other country before you call.
13. Note down all the important .... you're given by the other person.

3.2 Vocabulary

Before you do this exercise, look again at the expressions presented in 3.1 in the Student's Book.
Fill the gaps in these sentences and then add the words to the puzzle below – number 3 is done for you as an example.

1. Hello. This is Louise Bonnard .... Can I help you?
2. Could you .... the line for a moment, please?
3. I'll just call Mrs Sutcliffe on the intercom............... .
4. What is Miss Fisher's .... number?
5. Can I leave a .... for Sarah Grey, please?
6. Hello. This is Donna Marriott .... from Philadelphia.
7. I'm very sorry, I must have .... the wrong number.
8. Could you give me a .... tomorrow morning?
9. I made a note of her number in my ....
10. She's in a meeting, I'm afraid. Can I be of any ....?
11. Some public telephones take coins, others take ....

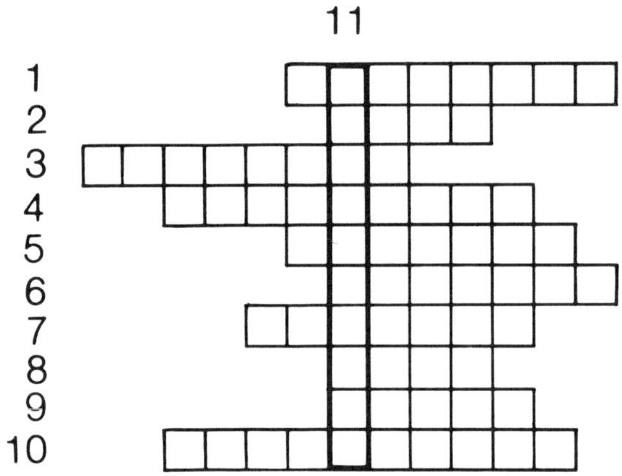

3.3 What would you write?

Functions

Imagine that you're writing a letter to a client. Write down the words you would write in place of the words given, which you might use if you were on the phone.

1. 'Oh, do you think you could call me about this next week?'
   Could ....
2. 'Do you think you could confirm this by telex?'
   Would ....
3. 'Sorry, but we can't give you a special discount.'
   I regret to say that ....

4. 'If you like, we can send you a sample of this product.'
   Please let us know if ....
5. 'Will it be OK to ship the order in two separate consignments?'
   With your permission, we propose ....
6. 'Thanks a lot for all your help. It was very kind of you.'
   Thank you ....
7. 'There may be some questions about our literature – if so, can I help at all?'
   If you ....
8. 'Terribly sorry, but you can't amend an order over the phone.'
   Unfortunately, ...

3.4 What would you like me to get you? *Functions*

First of all, look at 3.2 in the Student's Book.

Before you play the cassette, look at this example first – what you say is printed in **bold type** – then do the recorded exercise.

Colleague: I'm just going to the coffee machine. Would you like some coffee ... or a cold drink?
«beep»
You: **Oh, yes, please. Could you get me some coffee, please?**
Colleague: How would you like it: black or white?
«beep»
You: **I'd like it black, please.**
Colleague: Sure, OK.

■ ALWAYS ASK FOR THE **FIRST** ALTERNATIVE YOUR COLLEAGUE OFFERS.

You may need to pause the tape if you need to think before you speak.

3.5 Can you help me? *Functions*

To begin with, look at 3.2 in the Student's Book.

You'll hear some people making requests, offering to help you or asking for your permission. Agree or refuse, according to the instructions given on the tape.
Look at this example first – what you say is printed in **bold type** – then do the recorded exercise.

Voice on tape: Um, I wonder if you could lend me an umbrella? I need to go out for a little while.
«beep»
You: **Why certainly, I'd be glad to. Mine's over there.**

Pause the tape if you need to think before you speak.

3.6 Mr Brown, is it all right if I . . . ? *Functions*

Imagine that your boss's name is Mr Brown, and your own name is Chris. You need to ask Mr Brown's permission to do various things. Look at this example first – what you say is printed in **bold type** – then do the recorded exercise.

Voice on tape:	If you want to leave the office at 4.30 this afternoon, you should ask Mr Brown.
Mr Brown:	Yes, Chris?
«beep»	
You:	**Excuse me, Mr Brown, is it all right if I leave the office at 4.30 this afternoon?**

3.7 Present tenses *Grammar*

Before you do these exercises, look at 3.5 in the Student's Book.

A Fill the gaps in the sentences, using the verbs in this list:

assist *attend* *call back* *deserve* *get through*
look up *make* *pick up* *print out* *put through*

1. Normally she ....calls back...... straight away.
2. His secretary always .... the phone first.
3. This year we .... to get a pay rise.
4. This week he .... the Personnel Director with the interviews.
5. She .... the number in the phone book at the moment.
6. Today I .... a training session on quality control.
7. Once a week the computer .... the sales figures.
8. We hardly ever .... to Bombay so easily.
9. Please hold on. I .... to the Sales Department.
10. I .... some notes now and I'll make the call in a few minutes.

B Imagine that you're being given some information over the phone that you know to be incorrect. What would you say to the other person, to let them know they're wrong?

1. The parcel weighs 500 kilos, I think.
   Well, no, actually it doesn't weigh 500 kilos, it weighs 50 ....
2. You're making up the order this week, I gather.
   Well, no, in fact ....
3. I suppose the computer prints out the figures every day.
   Well, no, actually ....
4. You're working now as Mr Green's assistant, aren't you?
   Well, no, in actual fact ....

5. They always deliver the goods promptly, I believe.
Well, no, actually ....

3.8 Three messages *Listening*

You'll hear three messages which you are taking on behalf of your colleague, Mr Collins. Listen to the tape and fill the gaps in these notes.
After each message compare your notes with the answers in the Key – and then listen to the tape again to check again on any mistakes you made. Set the counter to zero before you play each message, so that you can easily find the beginning again.

1 SUSAN GRANT of Richmond Studios called about order for 1x MQ 20, sent 3 weeks ago – on .... of this month
Sent you cheque for £425 + VAT (i.e. £.................) to get it at special offer price but no .... of order.
Please confirm receipt of order and ....
Any problems, phone Susan Grant on 0303 ....
When can she expect ....?
Address: .... High Street, Woodbridge, ..., IP12 4SJ.

Look at the Answer Key before you listen to the second message.

2 PETER .... of Eastern Enterprises in .... called.
Can't .... on .... afternoon because of problem with hotel – no room because of ....
All other hotels in town full because of ....
Will come on Monday morning (............) if OK with you
Please tell him if this change of date is ....
Please call him if you have ideas for ....
on 617 ....

3 .... called:
Staying 2 extra days in .... and trying to get flight back on .... Direct flight is full – they've put him on ....
May not be back till ....
If not back, please take over at meeting on Tuesday with ....
All info in file on his desk with ....'s name on.
Please collect O.F. from .... Hotel first thing in the morning.
Any problem: leave a message at his hotel (.......................) or send fax (................................)

4 Reports and summaries

4.1 A company report

Reading aloud

This exercise gives you practice with stressed syllables when reading company reports out loud. But first of all, look through report 1.

Report 1

Océ has been in the reprographic (1)............... for nearly 70 years, manufacturing innovative (2)............... for the design engineering and office copying (3)............... . Today Océ is the world (4)............... in this market. In the mid-sixties, Océ first (5)............... the fast-growing copying market. And in the early (6)..............., Océ was the first European company to design, 7..............., manufacture and market its own plain-paper (8)............... technology. Our unique (9)............... was a response to buyer needs, bringing greater (10)..............., higher-quality output, exceptional user-(11)............... and operational ease.

Océ also entered certain segments of the (12)............... automation market, with highly (13)............... marketing and our own (14)............... sales and (15)............... organizations.

A Listen to the cassette. First set the counter to zero before you play the report, so that you can easily find the beginning again. Fill in the words missing from the report. (See the Answer Key for any words you didn't get first time.)
Wind back the cassette and read the report aloud sentence by sentence. After each sentence listen to the model reading on the cassette, then pause the tape and read the next sentence.

B Now read report 2 out loud. To help you to read it in a meaningful way, the report is reprinted below in breath-sized bits. The stressed syllables are underlined. Don't forget to stop briefly at the end of each line to take a breath. Let your voice drop only when there is a full stop.

Report 2

Groupe BULL is an international data processing and communications group with 26,800 employees in 75 countries, including a salesforce of 14,000 people, of which more than 5,500 are based outside France; it has modern manufacturing facilities (six plants employing close to 7,000), and a series of product families built around a distributed and open network architecture.

Groupe BULL is an international data processing and communications group
with twenty-six thousand eight hundred employees
in seventy-five countries,
including a salesforce of fourteen thousand people,
of which more than five thousand five hundred are based outside France;
it has modern manufacturing facilities
(six plants employing close to seven thousand),
and a series of product families built round a distributed and open network architecture.

Listen to the report being read out on the cassette. You may prefer to listen to the whole report before you read it yourself.

C Now read out reports 3 and 4 in the same way. The Answer Key contains the reports reprinted in breath-sized bits, with the stressed syllables underlined.

Report 3

The Swedish-based Electrolux Group is one of the world's leading manufacturers of household appliances. The Group also holds a strong position in world markets for commercial appliances, chainsaws and car safety-belts. Sales in 1986 rose by 34% to 53.090m Swedish kronor primarily as a result of the acquisition of White Consolidated, USA, and the consolidation of Zanussi, an Italian white-goods company. Despite extensive restructuring costs and an unfavourable trend for the U.S. dollar, income after financial items was maintained at the level of the previous year.

Report 4

Brown Boveri is a Swiss-based mechanical, electrical and electronic engineering company. Operating worldwide with 100,000 employees, it has factories, sales companies, technical offices and agencies in some 140 countries. Its main fields of activity are products, systems and installations for the generation, distribution and utilisation of electrical energy and the related automation, protection and control facilities. In 1986 sales increased to 13.8 billion Swiss Francs, and orders received to 11.0 billion Swiss Francs. Net earnings were 96 million Swiss Francs. Almost eight percent of the sales total is spent on R&D. Research topics include electronics, information technologies and process engineering.

D Now listen to reports 3 and 4 being read out on the cassette. Look at the Answer Key as you listen.

4.2 A report

Writing

Imagine that your managing director has asked you to investigate the health and safety provisions in your company's offices. These are the notes which you have taken, together with the recommendations which you were asked to make.
Expand the notes into paragraphs and write a report to your MD.

Begin your memo like this:

To: Ms Renoir, Managing Director
From: (your name)

<u>Office health and safety provisions</u>

1 As requested by the managing director on 30 March 19xx, I have investigated the problems which have been raised concerning office health and safety. In particular, I was asked to talk to

my tasks were (1) to speak to office managers and union representatives about how accidents or job-related illnesses happened and (2) to make recommendations on how best to improve situation

Results of study / all reported accidents past year.
three main causes
· faulty equipment – lack of servicing facilities probably responsible in two cases
· in several cases safety regulations not followed
· new staff ignorant of departments' health / safety procedures

In addition study all past year job-related illnesses reported.

also had meetings with union reps and office managers about what to do.

<u>Recommendations / Proposals</u>

1. should clearly display safety regulations in canteen and main offices
2. new staff need informing about safety regulations and policy
3. Personnel Manager responsible for instructing new staff on procedures for handling office equipment and for securing electronic / mechanical machinery
4. should practise first-aid drill at least once every 6 months
5. union suggested replacement of substandard furniture and equipment, especially
    1. old fashioned screens – cause eyesight problems.
    2. carefully check office lighting staff - complaints of headaches after work / lighting large part of problem
    3. essential to have chairs with full back supports - many staff complaints of backache

4.3 Using the passive *Grammar*

Before you do this exercise, look at 4.5 in the Student's Book.

A Rewrite the following sentences, using the passive form. Start with the words given and try to retain the same meaning more or less. The first one is done for you as an example.

1. They wrote the report in a terrible hurry. *The report...*
   The report was written in a terrible hurry. ....
2. Have you really checked the draft of that memorandum? *Has the draft...*
3. The temporary clerk finally found the notes under the filing cabinet. *The notes...*
4. We will produce the components at our Marseilles factory. *The components...*
5. We would reduce costs, if we used less paper. *Costs...*
6. You should note down all information in important conversations. *All information...*
7. They improved the memo to the staff committee in a number of ways to make it easier to understand. *The memo...*
8. They didn't include the mailing address in the letter. *The mailing address...*
9. You should make your suggestions in writing to the personnel manager. *Suggestions...*
10. They didn't put the call through, although we had asked them to make sure they did. *The call...*

B Rewrite these passive sentences in the active form. Begin with the word in brackets. The first one is done for you as an example.

1. The first automatic coffee machine was installed in 1982. *The firm...*
   The firm installed the first automatic coffee machine in 1982. ....
2. Further modifications will be made to this service for other customers. *The suppliers...*
3. The machines can easily be operated by ordinary office staff. *Ordinary office staff...*
4. The new generation of PCs can be placed comfortably on your desk. *You...*
5. The power, reliability and flexibility of computers has been increased by the microchip. *The microchip...*
6. Standard letters are now sent out a week earlier. *The department...*
7. Better results can only be achieved if you work harder. *You...*
8. The new note-taking method will be introduced in our office. *We...*
9. You should be warned about the dangers of not cooperating with the personnel manager. *I...*
10. All relevant information about the meeting will be supplied in advance. *The organizers...*

4.4 Punctuation

Read the following text. Decide where to add punctuation and to start new paragraphs. You'll also need to add some Capital Letters.

```
to managing director from staff training manager
date 18 october subject pc users introductory
course as requested i enclose a copy of the
provisional programme for the introductory course
for pc users it will be held from 16 december to
20 december following your secretarys telephone
call i have set aside a session for you to speak
to the participants i have scheduled this for
tuesday 17 december starting at 3 00 pm i am now
completing the final planning arrangements for the
course accordingly i would be grateful if you
could confirm that the proposed time on tuesday will
be convenient for you in addition i would also
appreciate receiving any comments you may have on
the programme by friday of this week if possible
```

4.5 Summaries and note taking *Listening*

Before you do this exercise look at 4.7 in the Student's Book.

A Listen to the cassette. You're going to hear two recordings: first a young woman talks about an experience she had. Then you will hear three people having a conversation.

First conversation

1. How do you think the person feels in the first recording? Why do you think this is the case?
2. Pause the cassette when you hear the tone.
3. Summarize out loud briefly what happened.
4. Start the cassette and see if the spoken summary is close to your own or not.
5. What other points would you add?

Second conversation

1. In the second recording, what sort of mood would you say the people are in? What is the reason for this?
2. Pause the cassette when you hear the tone.
3. Summarize out loud briefly what happened.
4. Start the cassette and see if the spoken summary is close to your own or not.

B Now listen to two more conversations. When you hear the tone stop the tape and WRITE a summary of the conversation using your own words.
Look at the Answer Key for a suggested answer. Remember there is no 'best version' of a summary.

4.6 Summarizing telephone messages

Listening

A You'll hear three messages. Each speaker has made notes of a phone call and is now giving an oral summary of the call from these notes. Set the counter to zero before you play each message, so that you can easily find the beginning again. Listen to the cassette and decide which set of notes goes with which message. Which sets of notes are left over?

1

TELEPHONE NOTES

DATE .... TIME ....
MESSAGE FOR A. Student
FROM Mr Takahito of Hamamatsu Electrics
MESSAGE Can move visit on Thu to 9.45. Meeting with manag. director 10.30. Ring back to confirm if O.K.
TAKEN BY ....

2

TELEPHONE NOTES

DATE .... TIME ....
MESSAGE FOR A. Student
FROM Peter Sheldon
MESSAGE Met representative in Kyoto. Should he stay further day? 2 factories still to visit. Trip to Toyota postp. till tomorrow. Visit works there. Will prob call end week. Please telex rep. Kyoto with instructions
TAKEN BY ....

3

TELEPHONE NOTES

DATE .... TIME ....
MESSAGE FOR A. Student
FROM Company in Paris visit next week
MESSAGE Re address 48, rue l'Abbé Grégoire in case delays TEL 43 57 46 35 Contact person: Silvia Monfort
TAKEN BY ....

4

TELEPHONE NOTES

DATE .... TIME ....
MESSAGE FOR Mrs Forsythe
FROM Raoul Lesage Lausanne-Dorigny
MESSAGE Re visit next week. Conference Tuesday. No one able to pick her up Geneva. Should take a taxi to her hotel. In case of problems ring 021/ 46 45 29
TAKEN BY ....

5

TELEPHONE NOTES

DATE .... TIME ....

MESSAGE FOR .. A. Student ....

....

FROM . P. Estrada from Toledo ....

MESSAGE Our switches not arrived ....
When? If non-arrival tomorrow .....
telex with further requests ....
pls call after receipt of telex ....

....

TAKEN BY ....

B Now you will hear three telephone messages. Listen to these calls and take notes.
Set the counter to zero before you play each message, so that you can easily find the beginning again.

1

TELEPHONE NOTES

DATE .... TIME ....

MESSAGE FOR ....

....

FROM ....

MESSAGE ....

....

....

....

....

TAKEN BY ....

2

TELEPHONE NOTES

DATE .... TIME ....

MESSAGE FOR ....

....

FROM ....

MESSAGE ....

....

....

....

....

TAKEN BY ....

3

TELEPHONE NOTES

DATE .... TIME ....

MESSAGE FOR ....

....

FROM ....

MESSAGE ....

....

....

....

....

TAKEN BY ....

4.7 Vocabulary

Fill the gaps in these sentences and then add the words to the puzzle below.

1. Put the name of the .... at the top of the memo.
2. Then send or .... the report to the person who asks for it.
3. When you take a message try to keep it ....
4. Your boss is an .... of the company.
5. Only .... the main points of a message.
6. Before you begin your report, ... or order the things you want to say.
7. Make a first .... of anything you write and then correct it.
8. Par. is short for ....

9. The .... is a punctuation mark with two dots.
10. Remember to .... your spelling before you type the report.
11. The punctuation mark that looks like a 'flying comma' is called the ....
12. When you report facts make sure they are ....
13. A letter used inside a firm is called a ....
14. .... is another word for *full stop*.
15. A .... is something that gets sent around to many people.

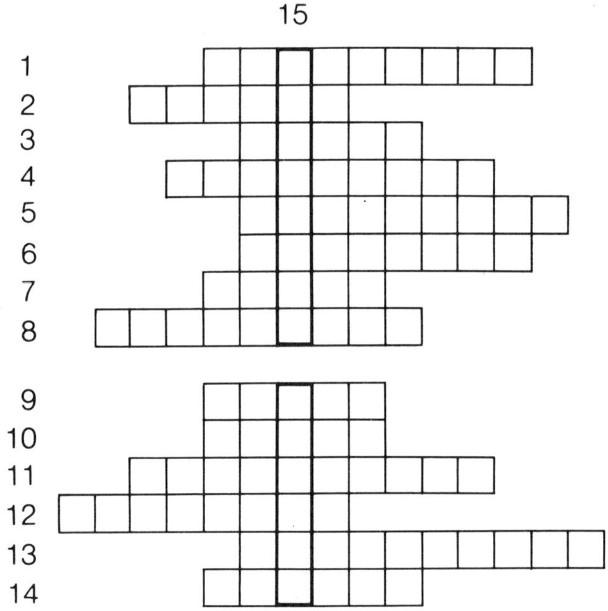

5 The place of work

5.1 Prepositions 1

This exercise gives you practice in using the right preposition together with a verb or a noun. From now on there will be an exercise of this type in each unit of the Workbook.
Fill the gaps in these sentences with a suitable verb or noun and preposition.
The first one is done for you as an example.

account for *advertise for* *apologize for* *apply for*
apply for *apply to* *approve of* *arise from*
backlog of *base on* *benefit from* *bid for*
blame for *bring up*

1. In the middle of the meeting our client ....brought..... __up__ the subject of compensation.
2. All reports need to be carefully written and .... ______ all the facts available.
3. The managing director was very satisfied: he .... ______ my recommendations.
4. If we want to fill the post, we'll have to .... ______ a qualified technician.
5. The clerk managed to .... ______ the two missing packages.
6. If you look carefully at your copy of the contract you will see that this rule .... ______ you.
7. Computer operators wanted. Please .... ______ the manager within.
8. The whole company is going to .... ______ the South American order.
9. So many people .... ______ the job, that we had difficulty in deciding who to select.
10. The authorities .... the multinationals ______ the inflated prices.
11. Such problems can only .... ______ bad planning.
12. The salesman .... ______ arriving late at the meeting.
13. The clerks had to work long after five to deal with the .... ______ orders.
14. Our agent .... $500 ______ the fire-damaged merchandise.

5.2 Agreeing and disagreeing

Functions listening

First read through the examples in speech balloons in 5.2 in the Student's Book.
You're going to hear four conversations in which a number of men and women agree and disagree about different suggestions.

Listen to each conversation twice. Set the counter to zero before you play each conversation, so that you can easily find the beginning again.

A As you listen the first time, write down the **topic** of the conversation or the **suggestion** the people are talking about.

B Rewind the cassette and listen a second time. This time decide which of the people agree or disagree with the topic or proposal.

Conversation 1

TOPIC: ....

	agrees / disagrees (put a √ or ×)
1st woman	
1st man	
2nd woman	
2nd man	
3rd man	
3rd woman	

Conversation 2

TOPIC: ....

	agrees / disagrees (put a √ or ×)
1st man	
1st woman	
2nd man	
2nd woman	
3rd man	
4th man	
3rd woman	

Conversation 3

TOPIC: ....

	agrees / disagrees (put a √ or ×)
1st man	
1st woman	
2nd man	
2nd woman	
3rd man	
4th man	
3rd woman	

Conversation 4

TOPIC: ....

	agrees / disagrees (put a √ or ×)
1st man	
1st woman	
2nd man	
2nd woman	
3rd woman	
3rd man	

5.3 Prefixes

This is the first of six sections on word-building. The others are: 7.4, 9.8, 11.7, 13.2 and 15.2.

New words can be formed in English by adding *pre*fixes to other words.

If you add them to other words they change the meaning.

e.g. organize → reorganize
copy → miscopy
standard → substandard

A Which of the meanings go with these prefixes?

mis- out- over- multi- pre- sub- re-

1. 'again' or 'back'
2. 'before'
3. 'below', 'under'
4. 'many'
5. 'past', 'beyond'
6. 'too much'
7. 'wrongly', 'incorrectly', 'inefficiently'

B Look through these sentences and fill the gaps with a word built from the word on the right and a prefix from the box. The first is done for you as an example.

mis-	out-
over-	multi-
pre-	sub-
re-	

1. The fall in the value of the dollar will mean a poor ..outlook.. for the tourist trade this year.	**look**
2. In the sixties many experts were warning that the population of Japan had ....**n** its resources.	**grow**
3. Because the machine had ....**ed** its usefulness, the production manager proposed ....**ing** it.	**live** **place**
4. The finance department badly ....**ed** the costings for the new factory buildings, so they couldn't be constructed last year.	**calculate**
5. There's something wrong with this bill. We didn't eat that much food. I think they have ....**ed** me.	**charge**
6. We've received so many complaints about the product that we will have to .... the next model.	**design**
7. Our major supplier is a large .... company, which always delivers on time.	**national**
8. We are willing to .... the labour between the two countries. We do the basics, you finish the goods.	**divide**

→

9. Most goods supplied to shops today are delivered in a ....ed state.	**package**
10. Industrial buildings are sometimes ....ed in Europe and sent to the Middle East to be assembled there.	**fabricate**
11. The problem with .... companies is that they rarely manufacture the components themselves. They always .... them to smaller companies.	**national** **contract**

5.4 Vocabulary

Fill the gaps in these sentences and then add the words to the puzzle below:

1. Several companies are .... in the development.
2. Ltd stands for .... company.
3. Hotels and restaurants are part of the .... industry.
4. Shops and supermarkets are part of the .... industry.
5. Our economy depends on private ....
6. The two firms want to .... to form a larger one.
7. We are moving because our business .... are too small.
8. The report shows our company had another .... year.
9. All the computer .... are linked to the main computer.
10. The .... joins the computer to the phone.
11. The .... department looks after the company's figures.
12. Another word for computer screen is ....
13. In America a large firm is called a ....
14. In American companies a director is called a ....

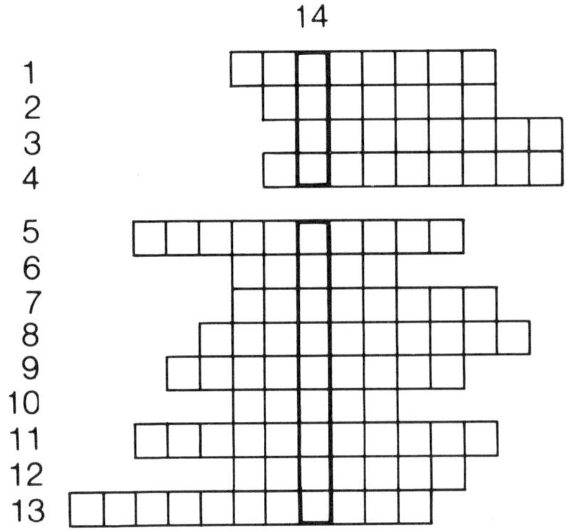

5.5 Referring to the past

Grammar

Before you do this exercise read through 5.5 in the Student's Book.

A Look at the notes on the backgrounds of the export staff at Biofoods International. And then complete the sentences below.

Biofoods International. HQ, Basel, Switzerland
Export department staff for the current year 1989.
Their present and previous position in the company:

Joanna: b. 1960 Binghampton, USA: 1980–1983 Business studies, Univ of Potsdam, Potsdam, New York State. USA: 1983–1985 Brown Electronics: 1986 joined Biofoods; since 1988 export manager: responsible for Scandinavia.

Renate: b. 1959. Karlsruhe, West Germany; 1979–1985 Economics and Computing, Univ. Munich; 1987 joined Biofoods as computer operator: 1988 trainee manager; February, responsible for Southern Europe.

Pierre: b. 1945 Amiens, France; 1964–1966 national service, French Army: 1966–1972 electrical engineering Univ. Nantes; 1973–1975 General Electronics San Diégo, USA; 1975 export salesman Atlantic Refrigeration St. Nazaire; 1977 joined Biofoods France; transferred to Basel 1980; Head of Export Sales since 1984.

1. *JOANNA* .... in Binghampton, USA.
2. From 1980–1983 .... at the University of Potsdam.
3. Then from 1983–1985 ....
4. .... at Biofoods since 1986.
5. .... as export manager since 1988.
6. .... for Scandinavia.
7. *RENATE* .... in 1959.
8. .... from 1979 to 1985.
9. In 1987 .... as a computer operator.
10. Since 1988 ....
11. .... since February.
12. *PIERRE* .... in 1945.
13. .... in the French Army ....
14. From 1966 to 1972 ....
15. After this .... from 1973 to 1975.

»»→

16. .... for Atlantic Refrigeration in Brest in 1975.
17. In 1977 .... and .... Biofoods France.
18. In 1980 ....
19. .... head of Export sales since 1984.

B Fill the gaps in these sentences with a suitable verb.

Example:. She ..'s been trying..... to get through to head office all morning.

1. Our company .... computers in its branch offices in 1988.
2. We .... very busy last week. I .... 15 orders on Monday afternoon.
3. When .... you last .... Madrid on business? Well, I .... never actually .... there before.
4. We .... just .... two new production plants in Paraguay.
5. Mr Miyagi .... for Toyota before he .... his own business.
6. .... you .... that telephone call? No, I .... able to get through yet.
7. After the plane ...., the customs men .... us waiting for an hour.
8. While the manager .... a meeting, I finished my report.
9. They .... a lot of correspondence, but the management still .... a decision yet.
10. While she .... in Stockholm, the company's Scandinavian sales ....

5.6 Asking for information on a company *Letter writing*

Your Role: You work for Light Imports, a company in the electrical light trade. You are given this advert by your boss and asked to write a letter to Luxor International.

Points to note:
1. Tell them your company works in the electrical light trade
2. Explain that your company is interested in knowing more about their company
3. Say you are looking for a partner in Sweden
4. Explain that you read their ad in a trade journal

Luxor International AB is an international group whose operations are focused on electrical lighting applications.

For information on the company and for a complimentary brochure outlining our world-wide activities and product range write to:

Luxor International AB,
Marketing Communications,
Lighting Division,
PO Box 673, Jönköping, Sweden.

5.7 Telework

Listening

A First listen to the whole programme and try to answer these two general questions:

1. What countries are discussed which have some experience of telework?
2. Did the individual teleworkers discussed have positive or negative experiences?

B Now listen to the programme again and complete these statements:

1. A consultant says that there are .... who work ....
2. He says the guarantee of success is more than anything else ....
3. According to the consultant the third major benefit is .... and the fourth is ....
4. According to the consultant the employee gains secondly, a ....
5. One problem for a trade union official is the possibility that ....
6. A person actually working as a teleworker says that one difficulty is that there is a need for very great adjustment ....
7. A woman argues that there are disadvantages for the employee, like lack of ...., the lack of ability to be .... and the lack of ....
8. A woman refers to a group of teleworkers who did this kind of work, because .... The other ....
9. On the future of telework, a woman says that being at home may not be the ....; it may not be ....

6 Import and export

6.1 Making enquiries on the phone

Before you do the exercises, look at 6.1 in the Student's Book.

A In this exercise you'll be calling Mr Chan in Hong Kong to find the information in the list below. Speak when you hear the «beep» sound. Look at the example first:

Mr Chan: Hello, Orion Electronics, Thomas Chan, speaking.
«beep»
You: **Hello, Mr Chan, I'd like to check some information about our order number 355.**
Mr Chan: 355. Yes, what would you like to know?
«beep»
You: **First of all, could you tell me how many . . .**

FIND OUT FROM ORION ELECTRONICS:

1. number of separate consignments
2. date of shipment of first consignment
3. expected date of arrival here
4. name of freight forwarders
5. and their phone number
6. dimensions of each package
7. weight each package

And tell them:
MR FIELD will be in Hong Kong next week. He'll call to arrange a meeting.

You may need to pause the tape if you have to think before you speak.

B Draft a telex to Orion Electronics, requesting the same information. When you have done this, compare your draft with the telex in the Answer Key.

6.2 What do they want to know? *Listening and reading*

A Imagine that you work at the reception desk in a large hotel. In this recorded exercise, you'll hear various guests asking for information – unfortunately, they all speak unclearly or quickly. Decide what each speaker wants to know and choose the correct alternative below. You'll certainly need to listen to each guest several times before you can decide. The first is done for you as an example.

1. The first guest wants to know if the time of the flight is ...
   a) 4:15 b) 4:50✓ c) 4:55
2. The second guest wants to leave a message for ...
   a) Mr Geoffrey b) Mr Geoffreys c) Mr Jeffrey d) Mr Jeffreys
3. The third guest wants to book some theatre tickets. He wants ...
   a) 2 seats on July 3 b) 3 seats on July 2
   c) 2 seats on July 2 d) 3 seats on July 3
4. The fourth guest wants to know if she can change ...
   a) to a double room from the 29th
   b) to a single room from the 29th
   c) to a single room from Friday
5. The fifth guest wants you to tell his agent in Greece to call him on ...
   a) 23983 before 3 b) 28393 after 3:30
   c) 29383 before 3 d) 23893 after 3:30
6. The sixth guest wants to know if there is ...
   a) a party for delegates at the conference
   b) a cheap party rate for delegates at a conference
7. The seventh guest wants to know ...
   a) Mr Wilson's room number b) if Mr Wilson is in room 405
   c) if Mr Wilson will be back at 4:05
8. The eighth guest wants to know how long it takes to get to the airport ...
   a) by car b) by train c) by taxi

B Now look at these extracts from correspondence. What does the writer want to know in each case?

1. Bearing in mind the difficulties you are having with obtaining components, we were wondering whether we might expect delivery of the goods during the next two weeks or whether there is likely to be still further delay.

   They want us to let them know ...
   a) what difficulties we are having
   b) what components we are obtaining
   c) when the goods will be delivered

2. In view of these circumstances, may we receive your assurance that, assuming we will not be receiving the shipment before July 2, you will be prepared to offer us a discount of 10 per cent on the quoted price?

They want us to let them know if we . . .
a) can give them a discount
b) will ship before July 2
c) will give them a discount if shipment is delayed

3. Would you be kind enough to inform us whether the price you have quoted for the units does or does not include a twelve-month service contract, which we understood to be part of our agreement with you?

They want us to let them know . . .
a) if we're providing a year's free service
b) how much our service costs
c) how much the units will cost

4. We would like you to provide us with a detailed specification of the machine so that we may consult our production managers regarding the suitability of the equipment for installation in our assembly plants. Please bear in mind that the power requirements of each unit are of particular importance.

They want us to let them know . . .
a) if our machines are suitable for their requirements
b) if we have consulted their managers about this
c) as much as possible about the machine

5. It appears that there may have been some confusion between your quotations ER889 and ER887 and that the quantities of the former may have been inadvertently entered in the latter. We would be grateful if you could check this and inform us if an error appears to have arisen.

They want us to let them know if there is an error in our . . .
a) quotation ER889
b) quotation ER887
c) quotations ER889 and 887

6.3 Vocabulary

Fill the gaps in these sentences and then add the words to the puzzle below:

1. After receiving their enquiry, we sent them a q.......... .
2. We have just received an i.......... for the goods we wanted.
3. Another word for 'buy' is p.......... .
4. A bill of lading and a letter of credit are both d.......... .
5. Please inform us when the cargo arrives at its d.......... .

6. We send a p.......... before making up an order.
7. Our agents will f.......... the goods to you when they arrive.

8. It's important to include the d.......... of each package on all the forms.
9. I've just heard that f.......... charges are going up.
10. That firm is our sole s.......... of these components.
11. They have added 15% for the s.......... charge.
12. When will you be able to d.......... the goods to us?
13. The r.......... price is 30% higher than the wholesale price.
14. Doing business on the phone with companies o.......... is very costly.
15. Before we can accept your order, we require a d.......... .... of 5% of the total price.
16. When fixing a price for an export order, the .... are very important.

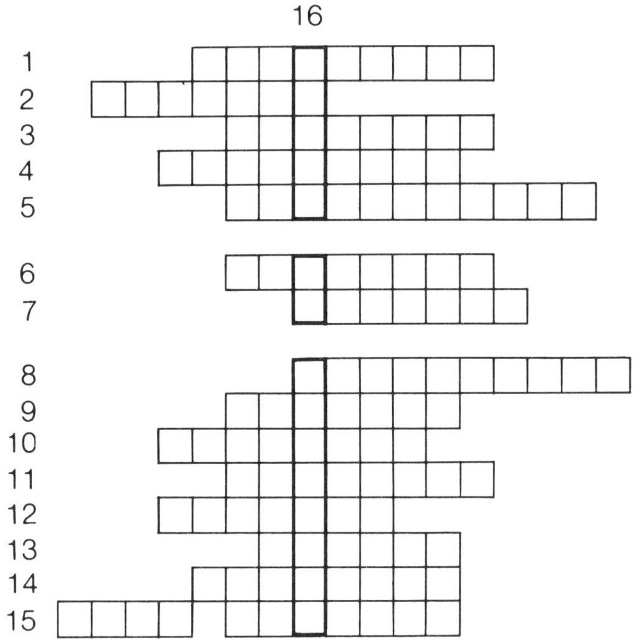

6.4 'J.I.T.' *Listening*

A Before you do the recorded exercise, look at this short list of 'golden rules'. Which do you think is the most efficient way of organizing a manufacturing process?

- Use your machines and workers as much as possible – they should always be working.
- Keep a good stock of products in your warehouse so that you can supply whatever your customers demand.
- Keep a good supply of materials in your warehouse so that you never run short.
- Don't run a machine unless you are making a product that has been ordered.

B Now listen to the recording. Here is a list of 15 points that could be made about J.I.T. – many of which you may agree with. Tick (✓) the points that are mentioned and put a cross (×) beside the points that are not mentioned in the interview. The first is done for you as an example.

1. J.I.T. stands for 'Just In Time'. ✓
2. Only a large company has enough influence and muscle to introduce J.I.T.
3. The J.I.T. philosophy was 'discovered' in the USA by Japanese engineers.
4. Workers are laid off when there are no orders to fill.
5. Capital tied up in stored materials is wasted.
6. Some products take weeks or months to manufacture – you can't apply J.I.T. methods to such products.
7. A machine should only run to manufacture a product that has been ordered.
8. Suppliers are at the mercy of large customers.
9. In manufacturing, materials account for about 60% of the running costs.
10. There is no point in making products for stock.
11. Employees must be fully informed of how the system works if they are to be required to use this technology.
12. Training and maintenance can be carried out if there are no orders.
13. Workers have to be trained to operate many different machines.
14. In bad times, suppliers have to suffer and lose money.
15. Suppliers and customers have to cooperate very closely.

C Now listen to the last part of the recording again and fill the gaps in this transcript. You'll need to PAUSE the tape frequently.

Interviewer: So, to come back to the supply of materials, this depends on the cooperation of your suppliers, then?

Expert: Absolutely! And changes in philosophy are essential here too. Most major companies obtain materials from over .... different suppliers. With J.I.T. this number has to be cut down to around .... The .... to the supplier is that he will get more .... from you if he can work with you in this way. Inevitably, this involves very close .... on the .... and .... of the materials he supplies and he must adopt the J.I.T. philosophy in his own .... If not, he'll find that the .... is on him to hold .... for his customers – and this will clearly not be .... If a supplier can't .... with J.I.T., then he'll find that ....companies will simply find other suppliers who can.

D Have you changed your mind about what you thought in A, now that you've heard the recording?

6.5 Prepositions – 2

Fill the gaps in these sentences with a suitable verb + preposition.
First try to do the exercise *without* looking at the list below.
So that you can revise later using these exercises, use a pencil to fill the gaps. Then you'll be able to erase what you wrote and do the exercise again another time.
The first is done for you as an example.

call on *capable of* *cater for* *collaborate with*
combine with *comment on* *compensate . . . for*
comply with *conclude from* *consent to* *consist of*
convenient for *convince . . . of* *cooperate with*
coordinate with *cope with* *credit . . . with* *cut back on*

1. I'll be ......call.........ing __on__ you when I'm next in your town.
2. If you suffer any loss, we will .... you ______ that.
3. He was unable to .... ______ the extra work and became ill.
4. The hotel is in the city centre, which is .... ______ the station and the commercial district.
5. We cannot .... ______ his taking a holiday at such a busy time.
6. I'm afraid I can't .... ______ another department's work.
7. As you appear to have been overcharged, we will .... your account ______ the sum of ¥600,000.
8. It is important to .... ______ any special Customs regulations.
9. Having studied the balance sheet, I .... ______ the figures that the firm is in serious financial difficulties.
10. If they have any special needs we'll try to .... ______ them.
11. This new design .... elegance ______ efficiency and strength.
12. During this project we have to .... our activities ______ our partners in the USA.
13. All members of a team must .... ______ each other.
14. We've been ....ing ______ that firm for several years.
15. Due to falling sales, the company has .... ______ its R & D programme.
16. They're .... ______ doing a much better job than that.
17. The cargo ....s ______ four one-ton crates.
18. She couldn't .... them ______ the need to redesign the product.

6.6 Air freight or road transport? *Reading*

A Which of these products would most likely be exported by air freight? Or by road transport? Or by sea?

bananas, computer equipment, cosmetics, whisky, books, meat, iron ore, televisions, furniture, toys

B Here are two interviews which were reported in a trade journal. Some of the sentences are missing. Decide where each of the eight sentences printed below fits into the spaces in the text.

Jane Harris:

We normally send all our exports by air now.

A ....

But we discovered that it didn't cost as much as we thought it might. This means we have less capital tied up in transit and as it encourages our customers to pay more quickly, this improves our cash flow.

B ....

And the packing costs are very low – we can usually shrink-wrap and palletize most of what we send out.

Our customers appreciate our using air freight: they know that they will get the goods in prime condition and promptly.

C ....

Surprisingly, perhaps, although the rates are high in comparison to other modes of transport (and these rates are standardized, so you can't shop around), the savings in insurance and packing costs help to compensate for this.

D ....

And because we can fill an order so quickly, our sales force can take an order from a customer by telex and actually get it to the customer within a few days of taking the order.

Bill Young:

We tend to use road transport for all our exports to Western and Eastern Europe, the Middle East and North Africa. We're a small company and our export trade fluctuates enormously. One month there may be just a steady trickle of orders and another we have enough to fill several 38-tonne trailers. Often, though, even the bigger orders are for a variety of destinations.

E ....

There are several reasons why we use road transport: first of all there's a very low risk of goods being damaged or lost in transit – that's because the driver accompanies his vehicle throughout the journey, and has to report in to his office during the journey too. He's personally responsible for the safety of the cargo, though, obviously, the consignment is insured against theft, damage or loss.

F ....

G ....

With our large orders we can get a swift, reliable door-to-door service with the trailer using a Ro/Ro ferry, so this means we can ship to a customer as quickly by road as we could by air freight – and at much lower cost.

H ....
Of course, the goods have to be packed well – though we don't use any special export packing. We don't find that the documentation or customs procedures delay our shipments either.

1. We started to do this because we wanted some of our products to arrive quickly, because they had a limited shelf life and our kind of product can go out of fashion quite quickly.
2. Our customer isn't going to appreciate it if he doesn't get the goods when he expected them or if they're damaged and he has to wait for replacements!
3. And the simplified documentation makes the procedures very much easier than other modes of transport – that's something my export staff certainly appreciate!
4. And because they're pleased and impressed, we can rely on them to pay promptly and we get a high proportion of repeat business.
5. Another thing is that there is almost no risk of part of any shipment being stolen or lost or damaged in transit.
6. Even with the smaller consignments that are collected and handled by the freight forwarder, we can get the goods to the customer quickly and in perfect condition.
7. The kind of product we supply is fragile – it has to arrive quickly and undamaged.
8. We use a freight forwarder, who can find space for small and large consignments.

6.7 The future *Grammar*

Before you do these exercises, look at 6.6 in the Student's Book.

A Fill the gaps in these sentences, using the correct form of the verbs below. The first is done for you as an example.

arrive *ask* *fly* *leave* ✓ *phone* *put* *see* *sneeze* *work* *write*

1. Will you be able to find out when the first plane to Paris ...leaves.........?
2. Tomorrow, I .... the boss for a rise and that's definite!
3. By the time I retire, I .... here for 10,000 working days.
4. She .... to Spain on Tuesday to meet our clients in Seville.
5. I .... the documents in the post to you first thing tomorrow.
6. Please don't disturb me for the next half hour, I .... Tokyo.
7. Excuse me Mr Grey, when .... you .... to our Norwegian clients?
8. While you .... in Stockholm, ... you .... Mr Olsson?
9. Stand back, everyone, it looks as if he ....!
10. Don't worry, I'm sure the spare parts .... soon.

➳

B Imagine that you're talking on the phone. It's a bad line and you don't catch some of the information given, shown as ~~~. Write down the questions you'd ask. The first is done for you as an example.

1. We ~~~ able to ship the goods to you on the ~~~th of next month.
   When will you be able to ship the goods to us ?
2. The plane from Bombay ~~~ here at ~~~ o'clock in the morning.
   When .... ?
3. She says she ~~~ apply for ~~~.
   What .... ?
4. I ~~~ stay here till ~~~, probably.
   How long .... ?
5. I ~~~ work this afternoon at ~~~ o'clock.
   When .... ?

C Imagine that a colleague makes a number of predictions that you disagree with. Write down what you would say to contradict him or her. The first is done for you as an example.

1. This will be difficult to arrange.
   Oh no, it won't be difficult, it'll be easy .
2. Our recommendations are going to be rejected by the board.
   Oh no, they ....
3. He'll still be working on his report at 5 pm.
   Oh no, ...
4. Tomorrow you start work quite late, don't you?
   Oh no, ...
5. I'm sure this machine is going to run reliably for a long time.
   Oh no, ...

6.8 Measurements

Vocabulary

One of the difficulties of dealing with the United States is that the old non-metric measurements are still used in some industries. Here are some common abbreviations printed in **bold type**. What do they stand for? Fill in the gaps in the puzzle below.

1. 1 **h.p.** = 746 watts
2. 1 U.S. **gall.** = 3.785 liters [but 1 British (imperial) gall. = 4.456 litres]
3. 1 **yd.** = 0.9144 metres
4. 1 yd. = 3 **ft.**
5. 1 **in.** = 2.54 centimetres
6. 1 **oz.** = 28.35 grams

7. 1 **cwt.** = 45.359 kilograms
8. 2.205 **lbs** = 1 kilogram
9. and, though not really a measurement, 1 **doz.** boxes = 12 boxes
10. Materials and goods are stored in a ....

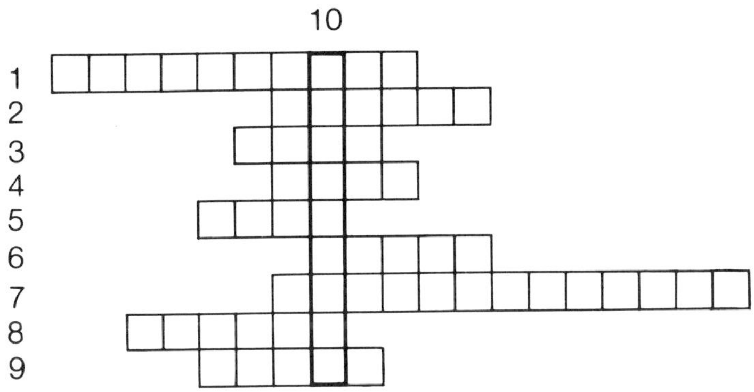

6.9 Thank you for your order . . .

Writing

Look at the letter below. Rewrite it as an individual letter to a customer – which would certainly be necessary if the customer had ordered *ten* items at this price and not just one.
The first lines are done for you below.

Dear Customer:

We regret that your order is being returned to you due to the reason(s) checked below. Unfortunately, prices of equipment are constantly changing and these changes are often not reflected in our advertising due to the months between preparing advertising copy and its publication.

Shipping and handling are also variable, so please include the proper charges if that is the reason that your order cannot be processed. It is always best to call us when more than one item is requested, to obtain exact shipping costs for your order.

From time to time items are discontinued and, though this is beyond out control, we will be happy to suggest products which are suitable. Please give us a call on our inquiry line (304) 739-8723.

Thank you for your patience, and we hope to serve you when the problem with your order noted below is corrected.

( ) Item requested is no longer available.

( ) Item requested is not yet available

( ) Invalid credit card number. Please check your card.

( ) Insufficient postage and/or handling. Please add $ ______ for shipping.

(✓) Price change. The new price is $ 145.75

( ) Other: ______________________

Additional notes: The product has been upgraded - the new version performs better than the original version, which has been discontinued.

- Begin your letter like this:

12 April 19--

Dear Mr Stafford,

Your order #767 999 for ten CX 99 processors

I am sorry to inform you that we have been unable to process this order and I am returning it to you for your attention.

7 Money matters

7.1 Reported speech

Grammar

Before you do this exercise look at 7.1 in the Student's Book.

Transform the conversation below into reported speech. The first part is already done for you as an example.

Anna Braun: Good morning! I'm just calling to ask about the second quarter shipment. Has it arrived yet?
Bill Armstrong: Well, I'm not really sure.

Anna Braun said she was just calling to ask about the second quarter shipment. She asked whether it had arrived yet. Bill Armstrong replied that he was not really sure.

Braun: Do you think it could have been delayed?
Armstrong: It's difficult to say. In fact I have no delivery note and no other record of its arrival.
Braun: Could it already have been delivered without your knowing about it?
Armstrong: Yes, perhaps. Have you already delivered it?
Braun: Yes. I already have our copy of the delivery note. According to this, it was delivered last month on March 15th.
Armstrong: I'm sure there's been some mistake. It has probably got held up in our warehouse or something.
Braun: Well the problem is that we've no record of payment. And that is the reason why I am ringing today.
Armstrong: I understand completely.
Braun: You've always been such regular payers in the past, haven't you?
Armstrong: Yes, I know, but I was just wondering if we couldn't have a little extension of credit, in this case?
Braun: I have to be honest. That would be very inconvenient.
Armstrong: But we have a cash flow problem at the moment. We have a large customer who hasn't paid for an order either. And we haven't budgeted for it happening.
Braun: I see.
Armstrong: Couldn't you possibly let us have just ten days? And then the cheque will be on the way.
Braun: Very well, but I must ask you to make absolutely certain that we receive it.

Armstrong: Even if we don't get paid ourselves, I'm sure we'll be able to get our bank to give us an overdraft.

Braun: I certainly hope so.

7.2 Numbers and figures

Reading aloud

A Read each phrase aloud and then listen to the model reading on the cassette. When you hear the number, pause the tape and read the next phrase yourself.

1. Around £250 worth of the shares on offer
2. You can apply for 100 shares at a cost of no more than £150
3. Sterling showed a 5-point gain at $1.3985
4. 58×72 cm
5. 44.5×17 cm
6. @ DM98 per 100
7. 26.8%, 47.2%, 29.9%
8. About £3.66 which works out at 19.5% per annum
9. 3¼″×2¼″
10. $2.2 bn a year, 1,700
11. 465,283
12. 10.75%
13. Invoice No. R3120/SCK
14. Invoice No. 007059
15. Tel. No. 0044 533 125697

B Now you will hear someone reading out the report below. Write down the numbers in the gaps as you hear them.

Profit before tax at .... was ahead by .... on turnover of ...., up by .... We must allow for the .... review of chemists' labour and overhead costs, as well as the net impact of currency fluctuations. Adjusting for these, profits were ahead by .... on turnover up by ....

Retail Division turnover at .... increased by .... and profits at .... were up by .... UK sales and profits increased by .... and .... respectively, before property disposal surpluses.

Industrial Division achieved sales of ...., an increase of ...., with profits of ...., ahead by .... At comparative exchange rates these increases become .... and .... respectively. The UK retail sales increased by .... from an unchanged sales area.

7.3 Request for extension of credit

Letter writing

Your Role:
You work in the accounts department of your firm. Your boss has asked you to write a request for extension of credit to Mr Ericsson, Dynamite Developments, Malmö, Sweden

GUIDING POINTS:
1. Refer to telephone call (14 June)
2. Explain reason for delay
3. Express your regrets
4. State intention to pay as soon as possible
5. Refer to dangers of bankruptcy
6. Promise to keep them up to date on developments

7.4 Suffixes

Word-building

A First, read through these notes.

New words can be formed in English by adding *suffixes* to other words. These are added to the ends of words. Some suffixes form adjectives which refer to the characteristic associated with the noun they are related to.

-al *-ary* *-atic* *-ly* *-ish* *-able*

When you form adjectives from nouns the pronunciation is often slightly different.
e.g. **national** /næʃənəl/ = relating to **nation** /neiʃən/

Sometimes the stress moves in the adjective:
e.g. **disciplinary** = having the features of **<u>dis</u>cipline**
programm<u>at</u>ic = referring to **<u>pro</u>gramme**

A further suffix:
fortnightly = refers to **fortnight**

Then there is this suffix which allows you to form adjectives from either adjectives or nouns:
e.g. **smallish** = fairly **small**
foolish = like a **fool**

There is one suffix practised here which enables you to form adjectives from verbs:
e.g. **controllable** = it is possible to **control**

B Fill the gaps with a suitable word, using one of the suffixes above. The first one is done for you as an example.

1. The opening of the banking complex will be an important commercial development for the region. **commerce**
2. Our customers asked us to pay our bills on a .... basis. **month**
3. The new model was up to date and visually very .... **style**
4. If you want cheap and .... products you can buy them at the discount supermarket. **afford**
5. The managing director prefers to leave .... affairs to his accountant. **finance**
6. The new range of furniture looks very .... **comfort**
7. The accounts department supply us with a .... list of all payments. **quarter**
8. When you retire early, you may receive a .... payment from your employer. **discretion**
9. Every company in our country is expected to contribute towards .... training. **vocation**
10. Last year's financial results show that it was a very .... one for the Group. **profit**
11. The new clerk was given some .... advice about dealing with customers who do not pay immediately. **caution**
12. Extra payments at Christmas are an .... feature of salaries in our country. **option**
13. For long-standing customers we have a .... rate of discount which is much higher than the normal rate. **concession**
14. Before we can decide where to buy our materials we require as much .... information as we can get on the suppliers. **statistics**
15. We required a .... description of all the company's orders since last December. **system**

7.5 Reminding customers of non-payment of bills

Listening

You're going to hear four telephone conversations. In each case a credit controller is reminding a customer of non-payment.
Set the counter to zero before you play each conversation, so that you can easily find the beginning again.

A First try and decide how polite or impolite you think each speaker is. Write the number of each conversation in the position on the following scales which you think fits best:

The credit controller is:

VERY POLITE	POLITE	NEUTRAL	IMPOLITE	VERY IMPOLITE

The customer is:

VERY POLITE	POLITE	NEUTRAL	IMPOLITE	VERY IMPOLITE

B In which of the conversations do the people sound friendly? In which do they sound unfriendly? In which do the people change their attitude?

C How effective do you think the calls were? What do you think the results were?
In which cases do you think the customers . . .

. . . paid next day.
. . . got an extension of credit.
. . . paid a week later.
. . . paid after a long delay.
. . . perhaps never did business with each other again.

D Now listen to the conversations once more. Which of these statements are true or false?

Conversation 1

1. the invoice has not been received
2. the customer usually pays punctually

Conversation 2

3. the credit controller 'apologizes' for calling
4. the credit controller is called Delaney
5. the credit controller says the terms are COD

Conversation 3

6. the credit controller asks about the April delivery
7. the credit controller speaks to Mr Roberts
8. the customer usually pays by cheque

Conversation 4

9. the credit controller asks about the April delivery
10. the customer says they have a cash flow problem

7.6 Prepositions – 3

This exercise gives you practice in using the right preposition after a verb, a noun or an adjective.
The first one is done for you as an example.

deal with *dispose of* *engaged to* *equivalent to*
give priority to *have a look at* *have a look for*
have confidence in *inferior to* *insure against*
interfere with *introduce to* *invest in* *involved in*

1. Company turnover has been so good that we shall be able to ......invest...... __in__ some new production equipment.
2. We are one of a large number of firms which are .... ______ environmentally safe projects.
3. This uncertainty about oil prices could .... ______ our plans for expansion.
4. The computers coming from the Far East are not .... ______ those manufactured in Europe.
5. At the company reception the new director was .... ______ the management by the MD.
6. The accounts manager asked the auditors to .... ______ the annual figures.
7. Our marketing department is encouraging customers to .... ______ their old machines and buy replacements.
8. If you're dealing with the French orders be sure to .... ______ the Duchamp order above all others.
9. The service engineer said he would .... ______ the defect. But he expected to take several hours to find it.
10. In many parts of the world the price of a car is .... ______ several years' wages for a worker.
11. Most enterprises supplied by BEC .... ______ their product.
12. Our overseas customers usually .... ______ damage or loss at sea just to be safe.
13. My secretary has just become .... ______ the personnel manager's son.
14. Our company has been ....ing ______ the same bank for thirty years now.

7.7 Vocabulary

Fill the gaps in these sentences and then add the words to the puzzle below:

1. Banks .... your account when you use a Eurocheque abroad.
2. Few companies pay their shareholders a regular ....
3. .... can result if your expenditure exceeds your income.
4. Our customers get reminders on .... payments.
5. People with large .... can always get credit from a bank.
6. Banks .... very high rates of interest on credit loans.
7. Suppliers expect their .... to be promptly paid.
8. A firm's costs include wages, interest and also ....
9. Despite paying our .... regularly, we still owe money.
10. We hope to increase our profits for this .... year.
11. Our profits were very small despite a large ....
12. The increase in .... will not change our price policy.
13. Every year a company must allow for .... in the value of its machines and buildings.

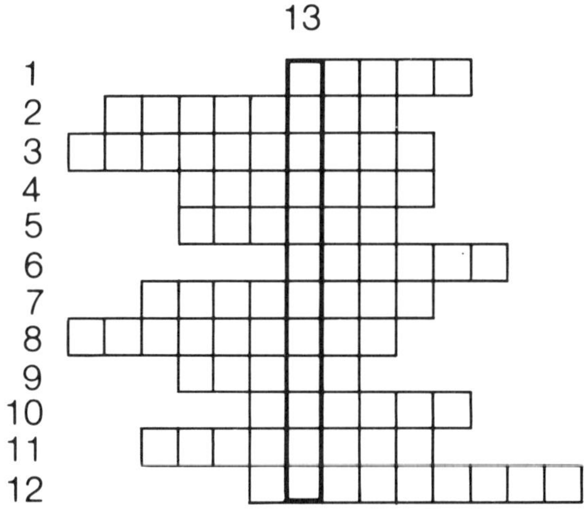

7.8 Taking a message – numbers

Listening

You'll hear four people on the phone repeating or 'reading back' from their notes the information, especially the numbers, they have just been given on some invoices. The first time you listen you won't be able to write down all the information! Nobody can! In real life you ask people to repeat the information on the phone until you have got it right. In this exercise, use the STOP and PLAY and REWIND controls of your cassette recorder!

Set the counter to zero before you play each message, so that you can easily find the beginning again. Then you can listen to the recording as many times as you need in order to write down the information.

Listen to each section, stop the cassette and fill in the relevant information in the invoice forms below. Then start the cassette again. The first invoice is partly filled for you.

1

1000111000111

Invoice No.
5968

Job Reference
1 77 205039

Marks & Numbers
(not given)

QTY	DESCRIPTION	Unit Cost

3

1000111000111

Invoice No.

Job Reference

Marks & Numbers

QTY	DESCRIPTION	Unit Cost

2

1000111000111

Invoice No.

Job Reference

Marks & Numbers

QTY	DESCRIPTION	Unit Cost

4

1000111000111

Invoice No.

Job Reference

Marks & Numbers

QTY	DESCRIPTION	Unit Cost

8 Delivery and after-sales

8.1 What's the problem?

Listening

You'll hear ten short phone calls. Match each call to these notes. Be careful, because some of the notes are 'wrong answers' and don't refer to any of the phone calls!
The first is done for you as an example.

1. a) The customer was sent only one set instead of three.
b) The customer was sent three sets instead of one.
c) The customer wants to be sent one set of three items.

d) The customer wants the damaged goods to be replaced.
e) The customer wants his/her account to be credited for the damaged goods.
f) The customer refuses to pay for the damaged goods.

g) The hotel has booked one double room for two nights instead of two double rooms for one night.
h) The hotel has booked one single room for two nights instead of two single rooms for one night.
i) The hotel has booked two single rooms for one night instead of one single room for two nights.

j) The speaker will arrive late because of the heavy traffic on the way to the airport and now expects to arrive at 1:45.
k) The speaker will arrive late because of delays at the airport and now expects to arrive at 4:45.
l) The speaker will arrive late because of the heavy traffic and now expects to arrive at 1:45.

m) The faulty machine has to be replaced.
n) The faulty machine has not been repaired satisfactorily.
o) The faulty machine needs to be repaired.

8.2 What would you say? *Functions*

Before you begin this exercise, look at 8.2 in the Student's Book.

What would you say in these situations? Write down the exact words you'd use. The first two are done for you as examples.

1. Your car wouldn't start and you have arrived a few minutes late for dinner with a client. What do you say when you arrive?
   I'm terribly sorry to be so late, Mrs Schmidt. My car wouldn't start.
   I hope you haven't been waiting too long.
2. Your train was delayed and you have arrived a few minutes late for lunch with some colleagues. What do you say when you arrive?
   Sorry I'm so late, everyone. My train was delayed.
3. You promised to call a client back yesterday but you forgot to. What do you say to him or her when you call the next day?
4. You misunderstood the instructions your boss gave you and mailed the wrong documents to your supplier.
5. You were given a copy of the sales figures by your boss, but you have mislaid it. What do you say to your boss?
6. You put the wrong date on the invoice you sent to a client. Explain why you are sending a new invoice.
7. You've been waiting 20 minutes for a colleague to arrive. When she shows up she apologizes, using the words in (1) above. What do you reply?
8. Your supplier hasn't sent the correct instruction manual, in spite of your reminder to him. What do you say?
9. Your boss promised to call your clients in Dallas this afternoon but it's now nearly time to go home. What do you say?
10. Mr King, a client, calls you and tells you that he thinks you have invoiced him incorrectly. What do you say?

8.3 Vocabulary

Fill the gaps in these sentences and then add the words to the puzzle below:

1. This is not a serious problem, it's only a .... fault.
2. We are rejecting the goods because we consider the quality to be ....
3. If you have suffered any loss, we will of course .... you for this.
4. We intend to .... for the additional expenses we have incurred.
5. You don't need a qualified electrician to .... a computer printer.
6. A number of problems have .... since we bought the machine.
7. The delay is due to a .... of qualified staff.
8. As explained in our catalog, this program carries a 90-day ....
9. As explained in our catalogue, this programme carries a 3 month ....

10. The engineer is on call 24 hours a day if there is an ....
11. There is a lack of .... for such an old machine.
12. We must have a computer system that works well, ... of the cost.
13. Their service department is responsible for .... the machine.
14. They are very .... about giving credit to new customers.
15. Any .... that is faulty will be returned to the supplier.
16. Please .... these faulty items.

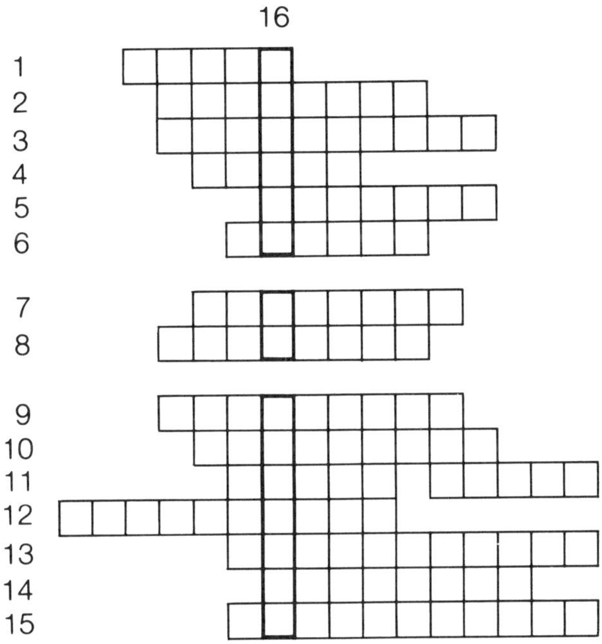

8.4 Only the best is good enough . . . *Listening*

A Before you listen to the recording, look at these opinions. Which do you agree with, which do you disagree with and which do you have no strong feelings about?

'Customers will pay top prices for a high quality product.'
'Customers generally prefer a low-cost product.'
'Nobody's perfect – we all make mistakes sometimes.'
'In every firm there are some people who aren't interested in improving the quality of the products.'
'You can't rely on workers to produce high quality goods without supervising their work all the time.'
'A company can't influence its suppliers' manufacturing methods.'
'Big companies can force smaller companies who supply them to obey their rules.'

B Listen to the recording. Fill the gaps in this summary of main points that are made:

The Quality concept can be applied to both the ....service........... sector and the .... sector.
Quality affects all the .... of the company and all the staff from .... level down to .... and employees.
The key idea is 'Zero Defects' – the company should be aiming to ....
Customers should be ....

IN THE PAST: goods were not .... to a very high standard. Some faulty goods reached the customer because a complete .... check of every manufactured item would have been .... Quality control consisted of ....

Customers ...., which could be corrected later by ...., who would .... the faulty goods.

NOW: people believe that Quality is important because:
a) Putting mistakes right is .... and .... It's more cost-effective to ....
b) If your competitors ...., your customers will prefer those. This applies to services too – your service has to be so good that .... and there are no complaints because of ....

You don't have control over your supplier, but you can .... to get .... This will mean paying more, but the extra cost is justified if ....

If you're getting poor quality materials from a ...., you may have to start looking for ...., or only accept supplies that are ....

To introduce Quality you must .... to everyone in the company. Everyone has to ....

.... can be trained relatively easily, but .... are harder to persuade about new ideas. Staff must ....
If the company can't sell its service or product, it'll .... and people will ....

8.5 I am writing to you . . . *Writing*

Imagine that you work for a company that has been receiving a lot of complaints from customers recently . . .

A Look at these extracts from correspondence your company has received this month:

```
Your service has been very poor

WE HAVE TWICE RECEIVED INCOMPLETE CONSIGNMENTS
```

I have sent you two letters and a telex, but received no reply

I have tried calling you several times but not been able to get through

Your products are excellent but your service is terrible.

We used to be able to rely on you to supply us promptly.

B Your boss, who is away on a trip this week, has left you these notes to deal with while he is away:

Please draft a letter that we can send to all our customers with the new catalogue.

POINTS TO BE MADE IN THE LETTER

1. Apologize for poor service (mention typical customer complaints):
   (a) ten phone lines, always manned, but once overloaded we can do nothing;
   (b) Correspondence staff working all hours to catch up.
2. Reason:
   Rapid expansion from small family firm to sizeable business. Working procedures haven't kept pace with expansion.
3. Last year old computer replaced with new hardware + software. We were told this would solve our problems but speed of processing orders slowed down. Last month new version of software supplied: system speeded up, catching up with backlog of orders. By end of month we'll be up to date.
4. Promise: orders will be delivered promptly + correctly; enquiries answered courteously + efficiently.
5. Actions speak louder than words:
   a) more staff now,
   b) new warehouse acquired,
   c) heavy investment in computer systems
6. End on positive note:
   we enclose latest catalogue, new product range more attractive + better value than before.
   Working hard to continue to improve service. Hope to count on your support in future.

C Draft a letter to your customers, perhaps beginning like this:

> Dear Customer,
>
> I am writing to you to explain the reasons for the very poor service we have given over the past few months.

8.6 What if . . . ?

Grammar

Before you begin these exercises, look at 8.4 in the Student's Book.

A In this exercise you'll see the replies to some questions. Decide what question prompted each reply. The first is done for you as an example.

1. How would you feel if you lost your job ....?
   Lost my job? I suppose I'd feel very upset.
2. How ....?
   Promoted? Oh, I'd certainly be very pleased.
3. What ....?
   A job in America? I'd try to improve my English as quickly as possible.
4. Where ....?
   A lot of money? I'd go on a world cruise, I think.
5. What ....?
   My own company? I'd pay everyone fairly and treat them as equals.
6. What ....?
   Tomorrow? I'd stay at home and catch up on my homework.

B Rewrite each of these sentences, so that they still mean the same.

1. They expanded too quickly and they couldn't cope with the volume of orders.
   But if they hadn't expanded so quickly, they would have been able to cope with the volume of orders.
2. They installed a new computer and things got worse.
   But if ....
3. The software was not tested and the system broke down.
   But if ....
4. Orders were delayed and customers complained.
   But if ....
5. The phone lines were overloaded and customers weren't able to get through.
   But if ....
6. There were a lot of problems and customers looked for a more reliable supplier.
   But if ....

C Fit these conjunctions into the gaps in the sentences.

if *in case* *unless* *until* *when*

1. We will be unable to supply the goods ......unless...... we receive payment in advance.
2. A spare axle is provided .... one is damaged during routine use.
3. The machine should not be modified .... a service engineer is present.
4. The filter should be changed .... the unit has been in operation for two months.
5. The red light will come on .... the machine overheats.
6. The machine should not be touched .... it has cooled down.

8.7 Prepositions – 4

Fill the gaps in these sentences with a suitable verb or noun + preposition from the list below. The first is done for you as an example.

lack of *line of* *look forward to* *merge with*
negotiate with *notify . . . of* *object to* *order . . . from*
place an order for . . . with *present . . . with*
put pressure on *proceeds of* *make a profit on*
proportion of *purchase . . . from*

1. He was presented... with a gold watch when he retired.
2. We've been .... ______ them over this since January.
3. We expect to .... a large .... ______ this deal.
4. We may have to .... ______ him to agree to our demands.
5. We have just .... ______ a new computer system ______ one of the major suppliers.
6. Unfortunately, there is a .... ______ technical information about these new processes.
7. What .... ______ our customers is completely satisfied with our product?
8. I .... ______ having to pay a handling charge to the freight forwarders.
9. Their firm has just .... ______ Apollo International.
10. Will you please .... us ______ any change to the shipping date?
11. We .... ______ seeing your new TV advertisements.
12. He spent the .... ______ the sale of the company on a luxury yacht.
13. What .... ______ business are you in?
14. We .... this product ______ a firm in the United States last year.
15. I think we should .... larger quantities ______ the suppliers next month.

8.8 Take a message

Listening

A Listen to the first of two recorded telephone messages. Fill the gaps in these notes as you listen. You'll probably need to hear the message more than once.

Call from .... S.A., Bordeaux.
• Both AR 707's running for 6 weeks now. Did usual routine tests before installing them in labs but now one unit is ....,
• Makes a loud harsh .... noise, as if drive motor is .... or one of the heads touching .... Happens .... times a day
• After .... noise stopped and .... normal.

→

- Question: is this a fault they ....?
  If it is a problem that needs fixing they can ....
  Please confirm that this will be .... and they can have
  ....
- Or they have unit examined by .... – ....
- Call him .... tomorrow a.m. on ....

B Draft a short telex replying to Mr Morand, explaining what action you intend to take.

C Now listen to the second message and fill the gaps in these notes:

Call from .... , ... Electronics, Toledo, Ohio.
- He's sent us .... and .... but no reply from us.
- Re: upgrade of 4 × .... Drives with new hardware options.
- He understood we would ship them at ...., then they would upgrade for ...., then ship them back to us at ....
- This arrangement .... in our fax to them of ....
- Problems:
  1. They've only ....
  2. We've .... for air freight and insurance
- Proposal:
  They will upgrade drive number .... and .... us for air freight and insurance. Please ....
- Question:
  Were other 3 drives sent at the same time?
  If so, maybe ....
  If not, ...

Call him tomorrow .... (.............................) or send fax (.................................).

N.B. If they don't hear from us, they'll .... and ....!

D Draft a short fax replying to Mr Santini, explaining what action you intend to take.

9 Visits and travel

9.1 Did I ever tell you about . . . ?

Functions listening

Listen to the cassette. You'll hear three people describing a journey they remember. Match these pictures to each story and put them in the right order:

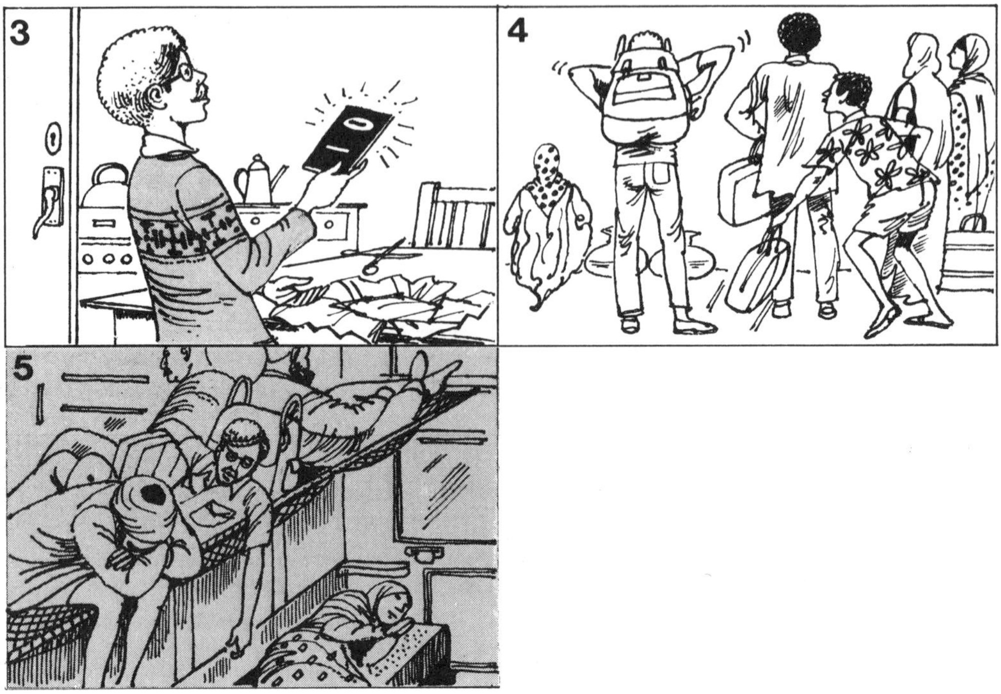
3
4
5

1
2
3

9.2 Prepositions – 5

Fill the gaps in these sentences with a suitable verb or noun + preposition. The first is done for you as an example.

qualified for *range from . . . to . . .* *reduction in*
regardless of *relating to* *remind . . . of* *remit to*
report on *report to* *resign from* *responsible for*
retire from *run short of* *run out of*

1. Please let us know of any changes in the law ......relating... _to_ patents.
2. That .... me ______ a funny thing that once happened to me.
3. She .... ______ the firm after 25 years' service.
4. He .... ______ his post after the scandal.
5. Have you read this .... ______ the West African market?
6. We're .... ______ computer disks – I'll order some more.
7. Please .... the sum of £750 ______ our agents in London.
8. We must achieve our targets .... ______ the amount of work we have to do.
9. He is not really .... ______ the job he has applied for.
10. Their products .... ______ paints ______ pens and stationery.
11. There has been a .... ______ the fares to the USA.
12. She is .... ______ making travel arrangements for the staff.
13. While I was abroad I nearly .... ______ money.
14. Jan and Pat both .... ______ Mr Brown, the export manager.

9.3 Air travel in the USA

Read and listen

A Before you listen to the recording, read this article from *Business Travel Weekly* and answer the questions in B below.

Hubs and spokes

Domestic flights in the USA are organized on the principle of hubs and spokes, like a bicycle wheel which has a hub at the centre and lots of spokes radiating out from it in all directions. One such hub is Houston in Texas: flights to over 100 other airports radiate out in different directions from there and half of these are non-stop flights.

For example, if you want to get from Miami to Los Angeles, you can catch a Continental Airlines flight from Fort Lauderdale (a few miles north of Miami and less hassle than Miami International Airport), change planes in Houston and fly on to Orange County (John Wayne Airport!) or Hollywood-Burbank Airport – both of which are much more relaxing and less crowded ways in to Los Angeles than the appalling LAX (Los Angeles International Airport).

The hub and spoke network has made flights cheaper and means that even quite small places are connected to each other by a major airline or feeder service. Another advantage of the system is that connecting flights are to some extent guaranteed. If one incoming flight is up to one hour late, all the connecting flights (up to 30 or 40) will be held until it arrives. So if you're on a delayed flight, that's good news – but it's bad news for everyone else because they all have to wait for your plane to land.

From the point of view of overseas connections, many hubs also operate as entry points or 'gateways', where passengers flying in from another country can join the hub and spoke system.

The same type of system does operate in other parts of the world: for example, you can fly from one part of Europe to another via Frankfurt or Paris or Amsterdam or London, but the difference in other parts of the world is that the fares are not any cheaper so there's no special advantage.

Flying in to the USA it's advisable, if you possibly can, to avoid any major gateway, such as Los Angeles International, Miami and JFK (New York) in favour of a smaller gateway like Charlotte, Pittsburgh or Orlando.

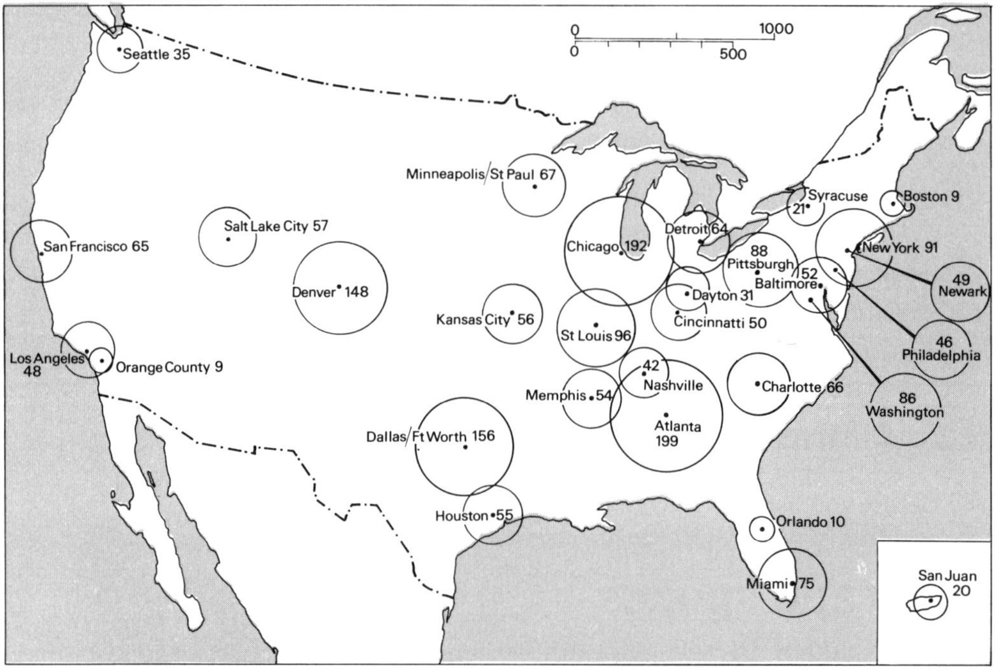

B Using the information in the text, complete each of these sentences. The first is done for you as an example.

1. If you want to get from St Petersburg to Los Angeles, you can . . .
   fly Continental Airlines and change planes at Houston, Texas.
2. If you want to avoid flying into LAX (Los Angeles International), you should . . .
3. If your flight is less than an hour late, your connecting flight will . . .
4. If you fly between London and Vienna via Frankfurt or Paris, instead of direct, the fare . . .
5. If you are entering the United States from abroad, you should . . .

C Now listen to the recording. You'll hear an interview with Nigel Isaacs, the editor of Business Travel Weekly. Using the information in the interview, complete each of these sentences:

1. If your flight is scheduled to take off at 5 pm, it will probably . . .
2. If you're sitting in a plane that hasn't taken off yet, you can't . . .
3. If your plane is flying round and round, waiting to land, you may feel . . .
4. If you volunteer to leave on a later flight, make sure that . . .
5. If you're travelling before a national holiday, you can expect that . . .
6. If possible, don't fly via . . .
7. If you have a small amount of luggage, don't . . .
8. If you want to be prepared for delays, take . . .

9.4 -ing v. to . . . *Grammar*

Before you do these exercises, look at 9.5 in the Student's Book.

Fill the gaps in these sentences, using the verbs in the list below with *-ing* or *to* . . . . The first is done for you as an example.

admire	*book*	*call*	*discover*	*drive*	*find*
get	*go*	*import*	*jog*	*let me know*	*make*
meet	*receive*	*see*	*smoke*	*stand*	*stay*
survive	*swim*	*travel*	*visit* ✓	*wait*	*wear*

1. I really enjoy ....visiting......... foreign places.
2. I'm looking forward to .... you in March.
3. It is essential .... formal clothes for a business meeting.
4. You can't get an APEX ticket without .... a month ahead.
5. .... on the left is much easier than some people think.
6. I dislike .... in line waiting to be served.
7. We can't afford .... at the Sheraton Hotel for a whole month.
8. I was relieved .... that I'd packed my traveller's cheques in my suitcase.
9. The plane didn't arrive early enough for me .... my connection.
10. I was pleased .... your postcard from Japan.
11. During the drive we stopped .... the view.
12. .... abroad in the summer can be very pleasant.
13. I expect you .... what happens at the meeting.
14. I asked them to stop ...., but they ignored me.
15. They encouraged me .... on a city sightseeing tour on my first day.
16. I managed .... to the airport in time to catch my plane.
17. You aren't allowed .... electronic equipment without a licence.
18. Why have you given up .... before breakfast?
19. In February, the sea is too cold .... in.
20. You must remember .... home to tell them you've arrived safely.

21. I think I remember .... her at the sales conference in January.
22. I don't mind .... here if you're not quite ready.
23. I'm interested in .... a nice local restaurant for our meal.
24. It's very difficult .... in a foreign country if you don't speak a word of the language.

9.5 What would you say?

Before you do this exercise, look at the useful expressions in 9.2, 9.4 and 9.7 in the Student's Book.

Write down what you would say in each of these situations. The first is done for you as an example.

1. Your flight to Charlotte is delayed. Find out the reason.
   Can you tell me why there's a delay on the flight to Charlotte?
2. You're booked on flight LJ 879 on May 16. You want to change this to ZZ 857 on May 17.
   ....
3. Flight RA 372 doesn't leave till 5 pm but you've arrived at the check-in desk at 12 noon.
   ....
4. You don't understand how to get a ticket from an automatic machine. Ask a passer-by for help.
   ....
5. Someone asks you how to get to the main railway station – tell him or her that it's two blocks down and then left.
   ....
6. You have arrived late because your rented car wouldn't start. Apologize to your host or hostess.
   ....
7. You don't understand some of the dishes on the menu. Ask your companion for help.
   ....
8. You want to order a plain omelette, which is not on the menu.
   ....
9. Ask your companion to recommend a local dish.
   ....
10. At the end of the meal you want to pay the bill, but the waiter has given it to your companion.
   ....

9.6 Vocabulary

Fill the gaps in these sentences and then add the words to the puzzle below:

1. You'll need a .... if you're going to the USA.
2. .... class is cheaper than Business or Club.
3. You can .... a car at the airport.
4. You can .... to a connecting flight without reclaiming your luggage.
5. He has .... his trip to the USA till next month.
6. What is the best .... to the city centre?
7. An American asks for the check, a British person asks for the ....
8. What grade of .... does this car take?
9. It's not my own car, it's a .... car.

10. I'm attending a .... in Geneva next month.
11. Can you get a .... to help us with this Japanese document, please?
12. Our visitor doesn't speak English, so we'll need an ....
13. How many .... will there be altogether at the congress?
14. What time do you have to .... for your flight?
15. The annual .... is held in a different city each year.
16. A charter flight is less expensive than a ....

9.7 What the clever traveller knows *Listening*

A How many of these tips for travellers are worth following, do you think?

- Never get to the airport too early in case the plane is late.
- Always take a good long book to read on a journey.
- Always try to get some sleep on the plane.
- Never take more than one suitcase on a journey.
- Always try to do some work on the plane – there won't be any phone calls to interrupt you.
- Never drink alcohol on a plane.

B Listening to the recording. You'll hear more advice from Nigel Isaacs (the man you heard in 9.3). Complete these sentences, using the information given in the interview. The first is done for you as an example:

1. You can avoid delays by . . .
   only taking carry-on luggage onto a plane.......................................
2. You can avoid losing any important documents by . . .
3. You can sometimes save money flying to Australia by . . .
4. You can sometimes save money flying to Rio by . . .
5. You will need a long time to recover from . . .
6. You'll lose efficiency and energy by . . .
7. When scheduling important meetings it's wise to . . .
8. If you make a lot of trips abroad, it's essential to . . .
9. A good travel agent knows which airlines to . . .
10. If you plan to travel with your husband or wife, it's worth . . .
11. You can save money on hotel accommodation by . . .
12. You can get special facilities at a hotel by . . .

C Now listen to the last part of the interview. Fill the gaps in this transcript of what is said by the speakers.

Presenter: I think the worst parts of a .... are having to .... or get up at .... to catch an .... flight, or being .... for a weekend in some dreadful .... city. Are there any ways of .... that?

Nigel: Mm, yes, a weekend .... or a .... in a more relaxing or .... city is often available at a .... cheap weekend .... Various airlines and .... offer these and it's always more pleasant to stay the night in a hotel than on a plane, even if you're in .... For example, for no .... you can spend an evening somewhere nice like ...., ... or .... before a .... - .... the next ....

9.8 Negative prefixes

A There are many different ways of forming negative words by adding prefixes. First look at these examples:

un-	fair	unfair
dis-	like	dislike
in-	visible	invisible
non-	smoker	non-smoker

■ Some adjectives beginning with **l**, **p** or **r** form negatives like this:

il-	legal	illegal
im-	possible	impossible
ir-	regular	irregular

B Complete these columns by forming the negatives of each of the words in this list. The first ones are done for you:

accurate ✓	agree ✓	capable	certain ✓	connect
convenient	desirable	employed	experienced	foreseen
formal	fortunately	honest	known	payment
profit-making	readable	satisfied	stop	sufficient
union	used	valid		

un-	**dis-**	**in-**	**non-**
uncertain......	disagree........	inaccurate....	....
....	....	....	....
....	....	....	....
....	....	....	....
....		....	
....		....	
....		....	
....			

C Now look at these examples:

anti- and **counter-** usually mean 'against':
anti-freeze   anti-American

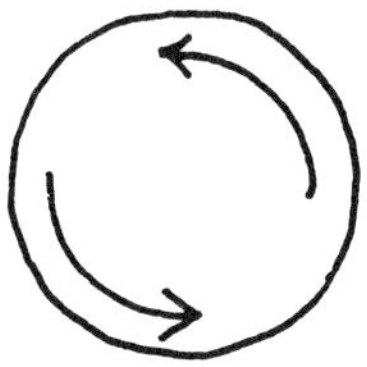

anti-clockwise (GB)/counter-clockwise (US)

semi- means 'partly' or 'half':
a semi-skilled worker   a semi-fast train

Write down words that mean:

against unions	....	not entirely official	....
half a circle	....	not completely permanent	....
against the government	....	partly automatic	....
not completely professional	....		

D Now fill the gaps in these sentences, using words from the exercises above. The first is done for you as an example:

1. The claims made in this advertisement are ..dishonest...... .
2. Please make sure you book me on a .... flight.
3. I'm afraid the deposit you sent us was ....
4. Discrimination on the grounds of race, religion or sex is ....
5. Please inform the manager if you are in any way ....
6. Tourism and financial services are .... exports.
7. Turn the handle .... to open the door.
8. Your visa expired last week and is now ....
9. ...., your reservation didn't reach us in time.
10. Due to .... circumstances, the flight has been cancelled.

10 Marketing and sales

10.1 Comparison

Grammar

Before you do these exercises, look at 10.3 in the Student's Book.

A Write down the comparative and superlative forms of these adjectives and adverbs. Use a dictionary if you're unsure of any of the words here. The first is done for you as an example.

1. awful	more awful	the most awful
2. bad	....	....
3. badly	....	....
4. basic	....	....
5. busy	....	....
6. dark	....	....
7. easy	....	....
8. efficient	....	....
9. fast	....	....
10. good	....	....
11. happy	....	....
12. noisy	....	....
13. pleased	....	....
14. reliable	....	....
15. serious	....	....
16. stiff	....	....
17. useful	....	....
18. useless	....	....
19. well	....	....
20. willing	....	....

B Rewrite each of these sentences, using the words given. The first is done for you as an example.

1. Our product is the cheapest on the market.
   No other product on the market is as cheap as ours. .
2. Our product is the least expensive on the market.
   All the other ....
3. There are fewer competing brands on the market nowadays than ten years ago.
   There aren't as many ....

4. One third of consumers prefer their product to ours.
   Three times ....
5. All other features of the product are more important than its colour.
   The least ....
6. Both the price and the design are equally important to our customers.
   The price is just as ....
7. Our product costs slightly less than theirs does.
   Their product costs a little ....
8. Their product is nothing like as attractive as ours, we feel.
   Our product is far ....
9. It's a bit more difficult to service the new model than the old one.
   It isn't quite ....
10. Their product is not as reliable as ours.
    Our product is ....
11. Our product is more widely available than most of the competing brands.
    Most of the ....
12. Price is not as important as quality, as far as our customers are concerned.
    Quality ....

10.2 Vocabulary – 1

Fill the gaps in these sentences and then add the words to the puzzle opposite:

1. What is the sales .... for the American market next year?
2. There's a full description of the product on the ....
3. We are about to .... a new product.
4. You can see the trend that these figures show by looking at this ....
5. The average .... is unaware of marketing.
6. This .... shows that our sales are rising.
7. I think you'll like our new .... on the wall outside.
8. Retail outlets are being encouraged to use this window ....
9. Not enough people are aware of our firm's ....
10. I think you'll agree that this new budget-price product is a real ....
11. Which of the .... should we place our advertisements in?
12. Our product compares very well with nationally advertised ....
13. According to a recent ...., 45.9% of consumers prefer not to buy imported goods.
14. The motor is exactly the same, but the case is a completely new ....
15. Which .... do our products sell best in?
16. Demand for many products may .... according to the season.
17. Thanks to our new ...., sales have gone up by 33%.
18. If you don't believe me, just take a look at these ....
19. You can buy this product in any supermarket or ....
20. Consumers must be fully aware of the .... of a product.

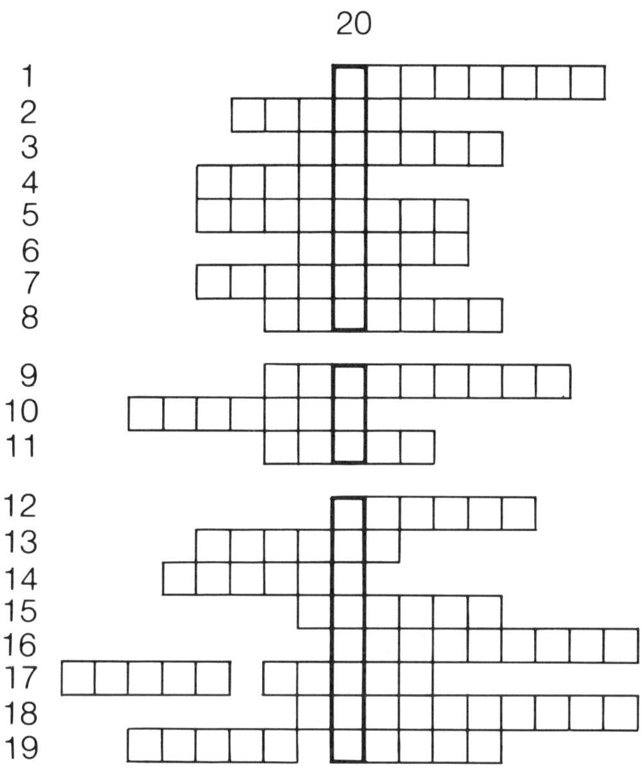

10.3 Prepositions – 6

Fill the gaps in these sentences with a suitable phrase from the list below. The first is done for you as an example.

scheduled for *share with* *specialize in* *speed up**
submit . . . to *subscribe to* *superior to*
take into consideration *take over* from* *transmit . . . to*
valid for *waste . . . on* *withdraw from* *write off**

1. Does anyone in the department ...subscribe... __to__ the Economist?
2. There's no point in .... money ______ radio commercials.
3. Can you please .... this telex ______ Tokyo?
4. One of the factors that we should .... ______ .... is the size of the market.
5. You should .... a copy of the report ______ head office.
6. I think we should try to .... ______ our contract.
7. We believe that our product is .... ______ theirs.
8. Is there any way we can .... ______ the process?
9. The meeting was .... ______ 3 o'clock.

* these are phrasal verbs

→

10. Can I .... some of this work ______ you?
11. Their agency .... ______ public relations.
12. This guarantee seems to be .... ______ every country except ours!
13. The whole campaign was a big mistake. We had better .... ______ all the money we have spent.
14. I'll .... ______ you if you need a break.

10.4 Vocabulary – 2

Fill the gaps in these sentences and then add the words to the puzzle below:

1. We'll send you a .... of our product.
2. How can we .... sales without taking on more sales staff?
3. I've noticed that there has been a .... towards ordering later.
4. There is an enormous .... market for this product.
5. ACME plc is our major ....
6. What .... of sales do you anticipate in your region?
7. We have built up a great deal of .... among our regular customers.
8. After that report on TV, we have had a lot of good ....
9. Even a company that has a .... invests in marketing and sales.

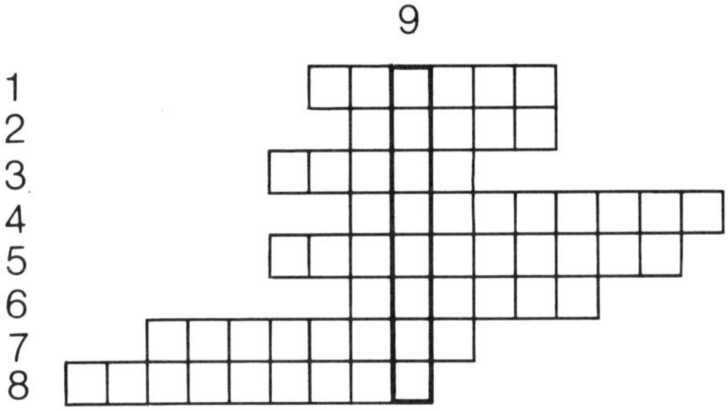

10.5 The three stages of a sales interview *Listening*

A Before you listen to the recording, fill the gaps in these notes:

If you want to be a successful sales person you should . . .

1. Know your .... and its main features
2. Know the strengths and .... of competing products
3. Find out who makes the .... decisions in your client's firm

4. Plan each sales interview .... it takes place
5. Match what you're selling to each client's .... and ....
6. Listen to what your .... tells you
7. Remember that each client is an .... , not a number.

B Now listen to the recording. You'll hear part of a workshop for people who have little experience of selling. Fill the gaps in this summary of the talk.

1. The .... Stage: usually a phone call. You have to talk to .... in person – not his/her .... Identify yourself and arrange an ....

2. The .... Stage:

   a) prepare and .... with a .... or ....
   b) dress ....
   c) behave in a .... manner
   d) don't spend too long on ....
   e) show that you're a .... person
   f) mention .... firms who use your product
   g) tell the client about the .... of your product
   h) encourage your client to .... and only talk .... the time yourself

3. The .... Stage: recognizing exactly when your client is ready to .... the order. This depends on .... Finally, ... your client for the order and leave.

C Now listen to the recording again. Which of these points were covered in the talk and which were not covered? Put a tick √ beside the points that were covered:

1. How should you follow up a sales interview?
2. How can you decide who will be a good prospect?
3. How can you judge the exact moment when a client is ready to place an order?
4. After receiving the promise of an order, what should you do before you start work on it?
5. What information do you need about a client before you go to see him or her?
6. How can you prepare to deal with a customer's objections?
7. Is it possible to rehearse a sales interview before you take part in the real thing?
8. How long should a sales interview last?

10.6 How certain are they?

Functions

Listen to the recording and note down the name of each speaker in this chart, according to how certain each of them is. The first is explained on the tape and done for you as an example:

A Was all the sales literature sent to Toronto?

100% (certain)	75% (likely)	50% (possible)	25% (unlikely)	0% (impossible)
Betty	Diana	Alan	Christian	Eric

B Is the new sales drive in Canada going to succeed?

100% (certain)	75% (likely)	50% (possible)	25% (unlikely)	0% (impossible)
....	....	....	....	....

C Will the new product range make a big impact on the Canadian market?

100% (certain)	75% (likely)	50 (possible)	25% (unlikely)	0% (impossible)
....	....	....	....	....

D Were the sales forecasts for Canada encouraging?

100% (certain)	75% (likely)	50% (possible)	25% (unlikely)	0% (impossible)
....	....	....	....	....

11 Meetings

11.1 What would you say?

Functions

Before you do this exercise, look at 11.1 and 11.3 in the Student's Book.

Write down what you would say at a meeting in each of these situations. The first is done for you as an example.

1. You're attending a meeting and someone makes a point you don't quite follow.
   I'm sorry could you say that again please? I didn't quite follow.
2. You make a good point at a meeting and want to make sure everyone agrees with you.
3. The meeting has gone on too long and you think it's time for lunch.
4. You are in the chair. You want everyone to vote on a topic.
5. You are in the chair and you want to go on to the next topic without a formal vote.
6. Another participant asks you to give your views on a topic you have no knowledge of.
7. You have given your views at some length. Now you want to find out if Miss Frost agrees with your proposal.
8. Mrs Collins made a point you agreed with a few minutes ago. Refer back to this before you give your own views.
9. Mr Davies made a really stupid point just now. Make it clear that you disagree, without being rude and provoking an argument.
10. The meeting is likely to go on for a long time and you're dying to go to the toilet. What do you say to the chairman?

11.2 About this meeting . . .

Listening

You'll hear two recorded messages about this meeting:

```
Meeting on Friday 13 April
10.30 to 4.30, including lunch
venue: Conference Room at Rainbow Products, Head Office
```

Imagine that you are Mr Hanson's assistant and that he has already left the office.
Make notes on the main points that are made. The first one is begun for you as an example:

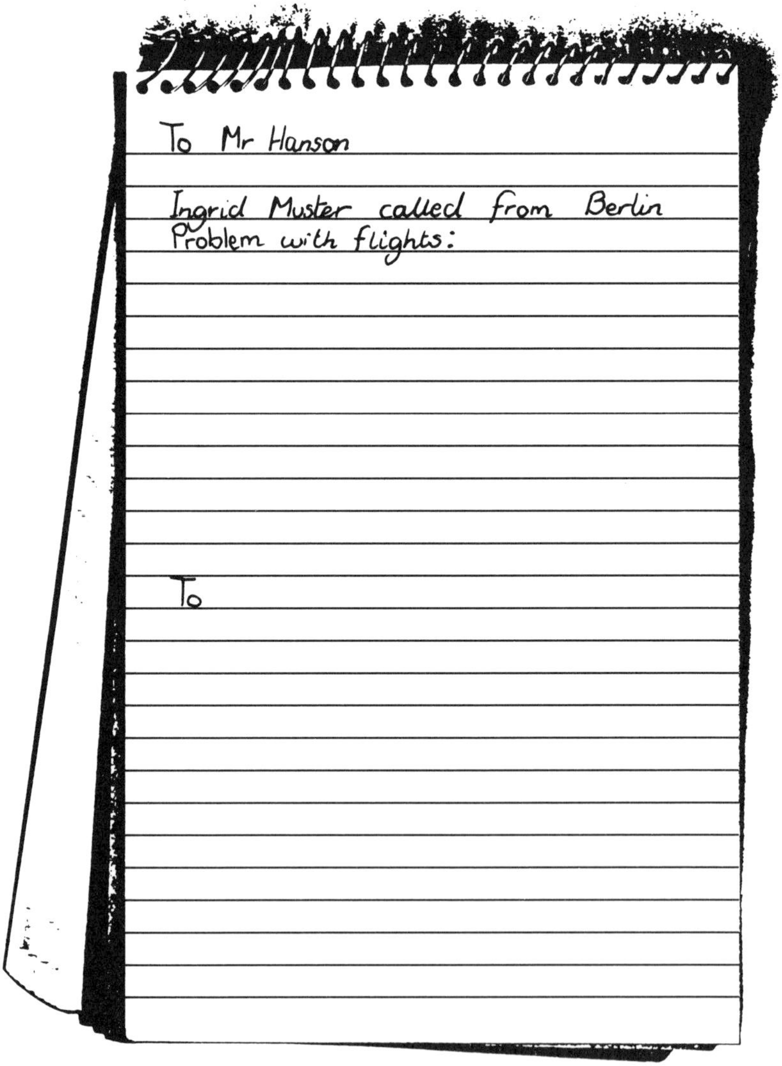

11.3 Vocabulary

Fill the gaps in these sentences and then add the words to the puzzle below.

1. Every meeting needs an ....
2. The secretary keeps the ....
3. A .... voted in favour of increasing holiday allowances.

4. A .... was passed at the meeting to approve the plans.
5. How many people are going to .... the meeting?
6. A meeting needs a .... to lead the discussion.
7. Before the main meeting we had a short .... meeting.
8. At 11.30 we decided to .... for lunch.

9. Mrs White will address the meeting on my ....
10. Let me know what the .... of the meeting is.
11. I have a .... to make.
12. A .... voted against increasing holiday allowances.
13. No one voted against – the decision was ....
14. Mr Grey has .... that we take a break for coffee.
15. There are a few more .... items to discuss.
16. Thank you very much everyone. I think that .... our meeting.
17. Is there ....?

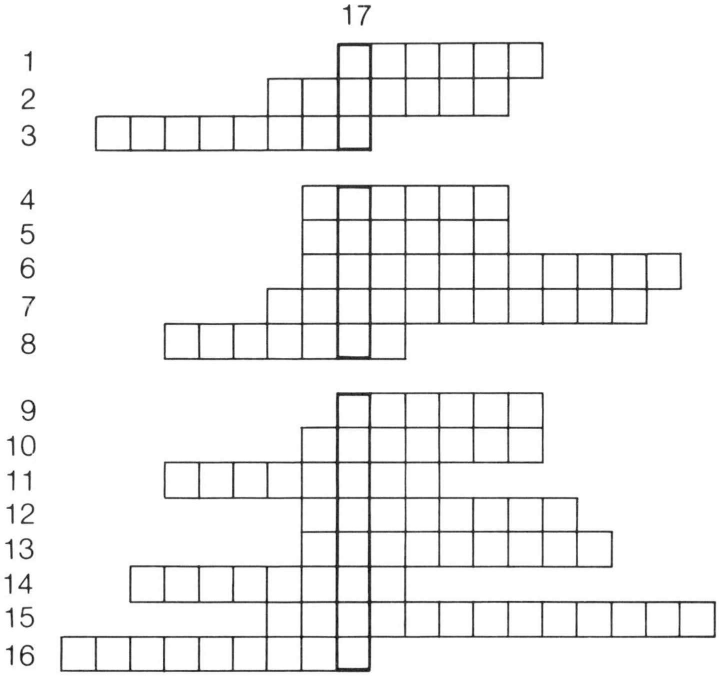

11.4 Prepositional phrases – 1

Fill the gaps in these sentences with prepositional phrases from the list below. The first is done for you as an example.

at a bargain price *at a good price* *at a loss* *at a profit*
at cost price *at last* *at least* *at our expense*
at short notice *at your disposal* *by accident* *by air*
by letter *by return of post/mail* *by telex*
during working hours *for cash* *for the benefit of*

1. We shouldn't change the venue of the meeting ....at....... such short notice
2. The letter we were waiting for has arrived ....
3. Our sales staff can be contacted .... on this toll-free number: 01 800 8071.
4. It wasn't done intentionally, it happened ....
5. Unfortunately, we were obliged to resell the goods ....
6. There are .... ten good reasons why we shouldn't do that.
7. Perhaps we could go over the minutes, ... the members who were away for the last meeting.
8. As a special favour, we can supply the goods .... plus 10%.
9. Because we are clearing our stocks we can let you have the old model .... of £14.99.
10. We can let you have the goods at a special discount of 7½% ....
11. Please reply at once ....
12. There's no hurry, you can let us know .... later in the month.
13. Please return the goods and they will be repaired ....
14. We can certainly supply you with these goods .... very ....
15. The goods were resold .... of 15%.
16. The components are being sent to Sydney .... and they'll be collected from the airport by our agent.
17. My office is .... while you're here.
18. Please send the documents to us ....

11.5 Place and direction *Grammar*

Look at 11.5 in the Student Book before you do these exercises.

Look at the diagram and write down exactly where each number is in relation to the letters of the alphabet and the sides and corners of the box. The first two are done for you as examples.

1. Number one is between the letter A and the letter B.
2. Number two is in the top left-hand corner of the box, near the letter C.

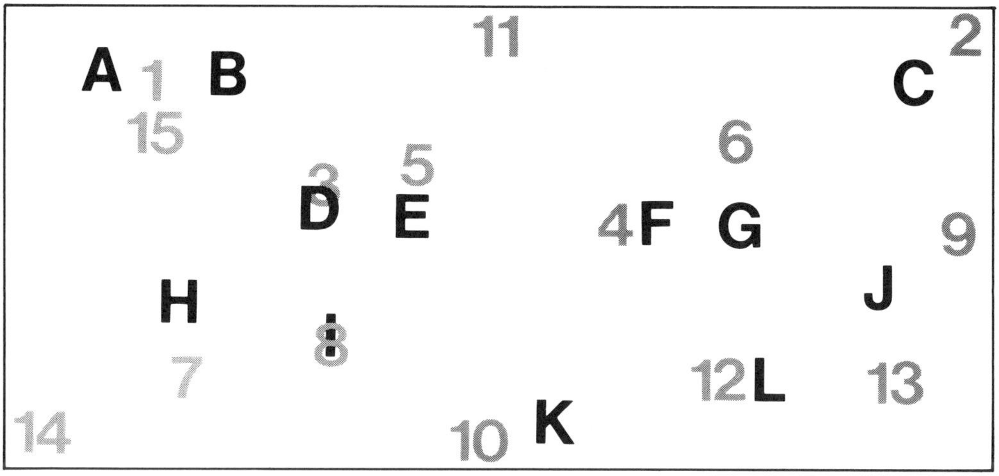

11.6 Choose the best summary *Listening*

You'll hear some extracts from a meeting of staff at Rainbow Products plc. Choose the best summary of each extract below. The first is done for you as an example.

<u>MINUTES</u>

1.
a) The consensus of the meeting was that 4,500 was a realistic target. One member disagreed.
b) It was agreed that 4,500 was a realistic target. Mr Green stated that he was not convinced. ✓
c) Mr Green said the target of 4,500 was not acceptable. Ms White disagreed.

2.
a) Miss Grey disagreed with Mr Brown that the new product range should be marketed in the same colours as before.
b) Mr Brown disagreed with Miss Grey that the new product range should include two new colours.
c) It was agreed that the new product range would be marketed in same colours as before.

3.
a) Mrs Scarlet agreed to investigate the cost of employing an outside agency to prepare publicity literature.

b) Mr Black insisted that an outside agency should be employed to prepare publicity literature.
c) It was agreed that publicity literature prepared in-house was not of a high standard.

4.
a) Ms Pink offered to draw up guidelines on the training of staff.
b) It was agreed that staff in some sections needed training in the use of the computer.
c) It was pointed out that Mr Gold's staff were afraid of using the computer.

5.
a) Mrs Bright agreed to prepare a handout on her staff's responsibilities and send Mr Dark a copy.
b) Mr Dark complained about the attitude of office services staff and asked for an official description of their responsibilities.
c) The matter of the attitude of office services staff was raised. Mrs Bright agreed to have a word with two members of her staff.

11.7 More suffixes *Word-building*

A FORMING PERSONAL NOUNS

An **advertiser** is someone who advertises.
A **supervisor** is someone who supervises people or a process.

Unfortunately, there are no easy-to-learn rules for the use of **-or** or **-er**. Here are some examples:

employer *adviser* *manager* *announcer*
treasurer *visitor* *administrator* *arbitrator*
competitor *creditor*

Now write the name of the person involved with these activities and then check your spelling with the answers in the Key. Use a dictionary to look up any unfamiliar words:

debt	....	negotiate	....
distribute	....	operate	....
examine	....	purchase	....
inspect	....	retail	....
insure	....	ship	....
invent	....	supply	....
investigate	....	wholesale	....
manufacture	....		

The counterpart of an employer (= someone who employs) is an **employee** (= someone who is employed).
Write down the counterparts of these people:

payer	....
licensor	....
consignor	....
employer	....

Note that two other suffixes are also used with similar meanings:

-ant

applicant consultant accountant immigrant
attendant informant claimant participant

-ist

machinist typist economist

B FORMING VERBS

If we **summarize** something we make a summary of it.
If we **pressurize** someone, we apply pressure to them.
(In British English, these can also be spelt summar**ise** and pressur**ise**.)

Write down verbs that have the following meanings:

to put something in a category	to ....
to introduce computers	....
to make a state industry private	....
to make a private industry national	....
to make something legal	....
to make a general statement	....
to give a subsidy	....
to have a special knowledge	....
to make something more rational	....
to make something more modern	....

If you **soften** something, you make it soft or softer.
If you **weaken** something, you make it weaker.

Write down the verbs from these adjectives:

tight loose hard bright flat sharp sweet

Note that we can also use the prefix **-ify** with a similar meaning:

classify qualify electrify purify simplify

11.8 We need some guidelines . . . *Listening*

You'll hear a recording of a one-to-one meeting about travel on the firm's behalf.

A Before you listen to the recording, look at the agenda of the meeting:

<u>AGENDA FOR MEETING ON APRIL 4</u>

1. Need for guidelines for anyone who's travelling on our behalf
2. J.L.'s trip to Germany:
   1. Expenses and need for advance to be paid
   2. Traveller's cheques + cash
   3. Meeting at airport
   4. Local people to be fully informed
   5. Itinerary: what details should be on this?
   6. Air tickets: check dates!
3. F.E.'s trip to Japan:
   1. Hotel problem
   2. Type of accommodation we'd normally book
   3. Club class or economy?
4. Any other business

B Listen to the recording and make notes on the conclusions that were reached, using the agenda above as your starting point. Don't look at the answer key until you have finished section C below.

C Write a brief report of decisions reached, that can be circulated to the people concerned.
Compare your report with the model report in the key.

D Now listen to the last part of the recording again and fill the gaps in this transcript of the meeting.

Kate: We haven't talked about the other problem that J.L. had: apparently his flight back had .... on it, the 24th. He didn't notice this till the 25th, the day he .... Luckily, the .... and they ....

David: Well, I mean, he should have ...., so ....

Kate: But this needs to be made clear. I don't know, maybe a .... when we send the tickets saying '...................... ....'

David: Very simple. Very, very good idea. We'll do that. And someone in your department must .... Do we need to make it clear that flights would normally be ....? F.E. seems to have the ....er.... F.E. seems to have the idea that ....

Kate: Well, actually, normally .... I think we should make this clear in the guidelines.

David: Oh well, I didn't .... I didn't even know that!

Kate: Right, anything else?

David: Er . . . no, I don't think so, but let's meet again when .... and ....

Kate: OK. Can you just switch off the tape recorder?

David: Sure, I press this one, do I? Like this?

Kate: Yes. That's right.

12 Operations and processes

12.1 Prepositional phrases – 2

Fill the gaps in these sentences with a suitable prepositional phrase.
The first one is done for you as an example.

in a hurry *in accordance with* *in addition to*
in advance *in anticipation* *in bulk* *in cash*
in charge of *in confidence* *in consultation with*
in contact with *in debt* *in difficulties* *in triplicate*
in progress *in running/working order* *in spite of*
in the process of *in time for* *in transit*

1. Could you please remain ....in contact with.... the head office, until the negotiations are completed?
2. While the firm is .... fitting the machinery the entire plant has been shut down.
3. May we ask you to pay the full amount due .... to our driver on delivery?
4. As long as the talks are .... the negotiating committee will say nothing to the press.
5. Please contact us as soon as possible if you find yourself .... Our representative will be only too willing to help you.
6. I am looking forward to receiving your shipment and thank you .... for your prompt service.
7. They ordered five more fully automatic systems .... the extra cost.
8. We are forwarding all the items on the list .... your request.
9. Most companies only deliver such items ...., as it is cheaper in the long run.
10. We have to request payment .... for all orders under $100.
11. We must ask you to take full responsibility for the goods, as long as they are ....
12. When we took delivery of the system everything was .... The problems have started since.
13. Our local agent will then make a final decision .... the regional director.
14. If the prototype is ready .... the exhibition, we shall give a demonstration of it.

15. We must ask you to treat this information ...., until the report is finally published.
16. Ms Andreotti has been .... our Rome sales office since last year.
17. Remember to fill in the invoices .... for the export orders.
18. .... the engines this factory manufactures the bodywork.
19. Although the partners were ...., they succeeded in paying our bill.
20. Their dispatch department packed the goods .... and forgot to secure them all tightly.

12.2 Explaining

Functions

Before you do this exercise look at the expressions in 12.3 in the Student's Book.

A Write down what you would say in these situations. The first is done for you as an example.

What would you say . . .

1. when you explain to someone you know fairly well how to switch a computer on?
   Watch. First you switch it on here. ....
2. when you are showing someone you know fairly well which button to press on a machine?
3. when you want to check that the other person understands what you've just explained?
4. if you want to add a further point to your explanation?
5. when you want to ask a stranger to help you use a photocopier which you don't know how to use?
6. when you want to ask a friend to show you how a machine works?
7. if you need a further explanation?
8. when you think you've understood what a friend has said but you want them to repeat it?

B Now listen to the cassette.
You're going to hear four recordings in which people explain how to use certain things or how to carry out certain operations. Set the counter to zero before you play each conversation, so that you can easily find the beginning again.

Listen and decide what it is that is being explained.

1. .... 3. ....
2. .... 4. ....

C Listen again and note down which words or phrases helped you to understand what was being explained.

12.3 Modal verbs *Grammar*

Before you do this exercise look at 12.4 in the Student's Book.

A Rewrite these sentences using a modal verb so that they mean the same. The first one is done for you as an example.

1. The Swedish company will possibly buy our company.
   They might buy the company. ....
2. It's possible for the firm to build the car at this plant.
   The firm ....
3. It is possible that is why the company closed down.
   That ....
4. We are considering enlarging the present site.
   We ....
5. The engineer suggested that we change the plan.
   He said ....
6. We suggest you try to follow the instructions more closely.
   You ....
7. The workforce is allowed to use this canteen.
   They ....
8. It is very important to follow the instructions closely.
   You ....
9. Plug the monitor in before you switch the computer on.
   You ....
10. It would be a good thing for you to listen to what your boss tells you.
    You ....
11. I think it is right for the company to pay more for overtime.
    They ....
12. It is not necessary for the assembly line to stop for them to do the maintenance work.
    The assembly line ....

B Now look at these sentences containing modal verbs. Decide which of these words has a similar meaning to the modal. The first one is done for you as an example.

not obliged *possible* *necessary* *perhaps*
possible *vital* *not able* *right* *essential*
perhaps able *not right* *important*

1. We have to buy a replacement for our computer.
2. We can't do it free, because the guarantee has run out.
3. I have to see the manager in person.
4. Couldn't the engine be repaired before the end of the week?
5. The customer does not have to accept damaged goods.
6. Regular customers oughtn't to wait for their service visits.
7. Employers have to provide their workforce with protective clothing.

8. I might finish the job, if I work overtime tonight.
9. The new department could open on the first of the month.
10. We need a fully automated assembly line, if we want to compete on the world market.
11. The plane might be late.
12. The travel agent should refund the ticket.

12.4 A memorandum

Writing

Look at this badly planned letter from the Chief Executive of a manufacturing company to his Production Director. Re-write it as a memorandum so that it is clearer.

Dear Jack,

This is just a brief letter to remind you that I would like to hear what you think about the set up for the proposed new machine shop. Our operations are going to be expanding in the next few years. Choosing the right machines for the new Machine Shop X is not going to be easy.

We require a new set of machines for machine shop X. There are a number of questions to be asked. Among them, the following: shall we buy, rent or hire equipment? I think we also need a clear policy on maintenance. How much regular maintenance is required to prevent breakdown of machines? Which as you know can be a very costly business. It is not good enough to wait until a machine breaks down and then fix it. At the same time we must be careful not to employ too many maintenance men. I mean, the machinery may never break down, but that might be even more expensive in terms of labour costs and wages.

And also, I would like your opinions on the speed of replacement. Could you please give me an estimate of how long some of the newest machines in the trade will probably last?

Cheers
Fred

12.5 How to fight noise

Listening

Noise is one of the major environmental hazards affecting our industrial societies – in addition to other kinds of pollution. And when it comes to work practices, the awareness of the dangers to health of high noise levels has been increasing in many countries.

You will hear part of a lecture given at a seminar on 'Noise in industry and society'.
The speaker is discussing a technique which is being developed in America to try to 'reduce' noise both in the working environment and outside it.

A First listen to the talk and try to decide which of these statements best describes how the technique which is discussed works.

1. Anti-noise removes other noises.
2. Anti noise uses the technique of 'muffling'.
3. Anti-noise creates vibrations which affect sound waves.

B Now listen to the talk a second time and answer these questions:

1. The speaker says that...
   a) the technology to make machines quieter has been available since the 1930s
   b) the method for making machines quieter has only recently been developed
   c) the technology for quietening machines has only now become commercially possible
2. The speaker mentions the fact that...
   a) American companies avoid spending money to get rid of noise
   b) American industry is affected by government regulations on noise
   c) The government has done very little against noise in factories
3. According to the speaker, American industry...
   a) is paying millions to compensate their customers for noise
   b) passes on the costs of noise to their customers
   c) does not follow the regulations because they are too expensive
4. Current techniques used to dampen down noise and vibration...
   a) are thirty or forty years old
   b) can result in the efficient performance of mufflers
   c) cause noisy components to suffer
5. The experts claim that the new systems can...
   a) deal with repetitive noise
   b) can eliminate noise completely
   c) can deal with one-off noise

6. The speaker describes a new technique using a microphone and a microprocessor which . . .
   a) responds to particular types of noise
   b) produces noise quieter than the car engine
   c) causes the car engine to run more quietly
7. The speaker refers to one area of application which . . .
   a) cannot minimize the noise of aircraft engines and helicopter vibrations
   b) would be able to reduce noise in the cabin of an aircraft to more acceptable levels
   c) has resulted in new aircraft engines that are noisier than earlier ones
8. Suppliers of electricity say that . . .
   a) generators should not be built close to where the power will be consumed – in cities and urban areas
   b) their turbines are affected by vibration
   c) they are cutting the amount of money spent each year on their transformers
9. Manufacturers say that they . . .
   a) cannot increase the speed of their production lines
   b) in general will also benefit from getting rid of or cutting down vibrations
   c) can control their production lines by using vibrations
10. According to the speaker, people working in loud workplaces with anti-noise . . .
   a) are affected by the effects of noise
   b) can work more efficiently in 'zones of quiet'
   c) can hear conversations from another part of the room

12.6 Vocabulary

Complete this puzzle using the information below.

1. Make easier
2. Another word for 'put in'
3. Another word for 'put in place'
4. Another word for 'stocks and supplies'
5. Make more simple and more effective
6. This can stop you finishing the job
7. If you take a machine to pieces you do this
8. Something manufactured without intention

9. Another word for change
10. Keeping machines in good order
11. Opposite of reduce
12. Another word for workforce

13. A place used to manufacture things

13 A new job

13.1 Looking for a job

Reading aloud

Look at these two advertisements and prepare to read them aloud.

1. Decide where you will pause as you're reading them. Decide how you will pronounce any unfamiliar words and all the numbers.
2. Read each advertisement aloud. If possible, record your own reading on a separate blank tape, so that you can get an idea of how you sound.
3. Then compare your reading with the model readings on the cassette.
4. After hearing the model readings, read each passage aloud again and record your reading.

JOB HUNTING?

Did you know that the best jobs are not advertised – even in this newspaper?

That's why our employment service can help you to find the job you deserve.

Our president and staff have over 200 years of experience in placing people like you in jobs. We have contacts with every major corporation and public service in this area.

If you are frustrated with your present job or presently unemployed, call us for an appointment or send us your resumé today. No cost or obligation, total confidentiality. We promise you that we will offer you friendly, realistic and professional advice in your job search. We have a fine record of success in helping people like you, so why not let us share our success with you?

JOB HUNTERS, INC
461 Ocean Boulevard, Santa Barbara, CA 93102
235 9860

EFFECTIVE JOB SEARCHING
— CVs à la carte

To get the right job you need to be attractive to employers from the moment they first hear about you. We specialize in thoroughly preparing professional people for effective job searching.

Our confidential and professional service includes:

- a personal interview with one of our qualified counsellors,
- advice and training in approaching employers,
- all application letters prepared and professionally typed for you,
- an individually-prepared CV that emphasizes your achievements,
- training in interview techniques.

Our service will ensure that employers put you on their short list and that you present yourself positively and effectively at the interview.

SUSAN BRIGHT CVs
891 New Oxford Street, London WC1T 8JK
01-997 8091

13.2 Abstract nouns

Word-building

Use a dictionary to look up any unfamiliar words in these exercises.

A VERBS → NOUNS
Abstract nouns can be formed from many verbs in English by adding **-ment** or **-tion**. Look at these examples:

-ment

manage	management
improve	improvement

-tion

connect	connection
classify	classification
duplicate	duplication
educate	education

What are the noun forms of these verbs? Only write down the ones which are unfamiliar or which you're unsure of.

acknowledge, achieve, adjourn, agree, announce, amend, arrange, assess, consign, develop, embarrass, endorse, enjoy, equip, establish, judge, measure, repay

adapt, alter, apply, authorize, centralize, cancel, confirm, consult, declare, determine, devalue, imagine, modify, pronounce, recommend, specialize

administrate, appreciate, arbitrate, automate, circulate, collaborate, cooperate, complicate, concentrate, calculate, eliminate, fluctuate, hesitate, integrate, locate, speculate

attract, collect, contribute, correct, deduct, delete, interrupt, pollute, predict, protect, reduce

Abstract nouns are formed from some verbs by adding **-al** or **-ance**. Here are some examples:

-al

arrive	arrival
withdraw	withdrawal
refuse	refusal

-ance

accept	acceptance
appear	appearance
assist	assistance
perform	performance

B ADJECTIVES → NOUNS

Nouns can be formed from adjectives by adding **-ness**, **-ence** or **-ity**. Look at these examples:

-ness

aware	awareness
bright	brightness

-ity

able	ability
available	availability

-ence

negligent	negligence
insistent	insistence

What are the noun forms of these adjectives? Only write down the ones which are unfamiliar or which you're unsure of.

calm, careless, cheap, friendly, helpful, late, loud, nervous, serious

confident, intelligent, patient, different

capable, flexible, formal, inferior, legal, objective, possible, probable, popular, real, reliable, scarce, sincere, superior

13.3 An interesting job

Writing

Imagine that you are interested in applying for this job. You have heard of ACME Atlantic and your own firm has done business with them. You know that you can get leave of absence from your own company for up to 9 months – or you are not currently employed. Write a letter applying for the job, which you will send to support your application with your CV/resumé. You have already made some notes on the points you want to make in your application letter.

WORK IN BERMUDA!

ACME Atlantic are a well-known and respected trading company. We handle imports directly from manufacturers in 35 different countries, often to our own specifications, and currently export to 46 different countries worldwide.

We are looking for enthusiastic people to work in our office in Bermuda on temporary 3-, 6- and 9- month contracts. Applicants must be able to speak and write at least one foreign language fluently and can be nationals of any country.

Experience in import/export will be an advantage, but as special training will be available this is not essential. The main requirements are a willingness to work as a member of a team, to cope with pressure, to use the telephone in a foreign language and in English and to be prepared occasionally to work long hours when necessary.

There are several posts available and long-term prospects are good, though initially all successful applicants will be contracted for a maximum of 9 months.

The salary we will offer is excellent. We will pay for your return air fare and provide adequate accommodation at a nominal rent.

Please apply in your own handwriting, enclosing your resumé, to Charles Fox, European Sales Office, ACME Atlantic Ltd, 45 Pentonville Road, London EC2 4AC.

NOTES

1. Introduce myself: name, age, nationality, etc.
2. Mention my company's contact with ACME.
3. Say what length contract I'd be interested in.
4. Describe relevant experience – or justify lack of experience.
5. Describe my skills in my own and other languages.
6. Describe how I meet the requirements of the job.
7. Say when I'm available for interview.

13.4 Relative clauses

Grammar

A Fill the gaps in these sentences with a suitable relative pronoun. Add any commas that are missing. The first is done for you as an example.

1. The person .....who.... impressed me most was Mr Wright. (no commas)
2. Mr Wright .... application form we received yesterday is a very promising candidate.
3. His CV .... you showed me yesterday is most impressive.
4. He has excellent references from his present employers .... are ACME Engineering.
5. He was working in Norwich .... they have their HQ.
6. His qualifications .... you commented on are excellent.
7. The personnel officer .... interviewed him says that he's available at once.
8. The thing .... impressed her most is his personality.

B Make each of these pairs of sentences into a single sentence, using a relative pronoun. The first is done for you as an example.

1. He told us about his experiences in India. This was interesting.
   He told us about his experiences in India, which was interesting.
2. I heard about the vacancy from a friend. This friend works in Personnel.
   ....
3. He gave me some information. This information was supposed to be confidential.
   ....
4. I heard about this from a colleague. This colleague assured me it was true.
   ....
5. Apparently, we sent the forms to an address. This address was wrong.
   ....
6. You gave a person's name as a reference. This person is unwilling to comment on you.
   ....
7. I had to fill in a six-page application form. This was very time-consuming.
   ....
8. I applied for a job. I saw this job advertised in the newspaper.
   ....

13.5 Vocabulary

Fill the gaps in these sentences, then add the words to the puzzle below.

1. In American English, you .... an application form.
2. She's going to make engineering her ....
3. Are we going to .... a new sales manager?
4. He was the most promising .... for the job.
5. The past tense of *seek* is ....
6. All our production workers are paid top ....
7. The applicants will be interviewed by the .... of directors.
8. Mr and Mrs Smith supplement their .... by renting out rooms.
9. A well-prepared .... will do well at any interview.
10. The applicants were interviewed by a .... of three managers.
11. If you're .... – .... you're your own boss.
12. Could you explain to me what the .... of the job are?
13. How much .... will I have to pay?
14. What is your present annual ....?
15. A company car, subsidized meals or low-interest loans are all ....

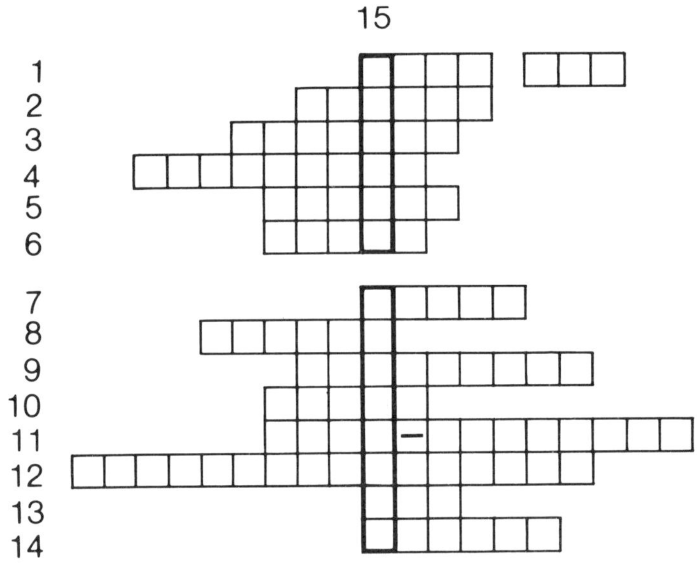

16. What will be my .... in the company, in relation to other employees?
17. When you retire, you'll receive a good ....
18. After working part-time, she's now seeking a .... job.
19. What are the .... for promotion within the company?
20. I'm looking for a new .... in a more demanding job.
21. All job applications are handled by the .... department.

22. We need a .... replacement for her, while she's on maternity leave.
23. In British English, you .... a form.
24. Most secondary schools offer their students .... guidance before they leave.
25. An American firm will ask you to send a .... with your application form.
26. To enter a skilled job in some countries, you have to serve some years as an .... first.

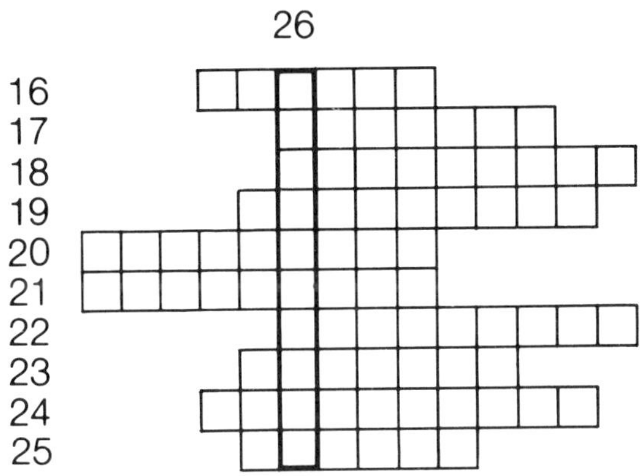

13.6 Who should we short-list?

Listening

A Before you listen to the recording, look at this advertisement. Each of the speakers you'll hear has held interviews with applicants for this job:

ASSISTANT MARKETING MANAGER

We are a well-known international manufacturer, based in the UK, and we are expanding our export marketing activities in our European headquarters in London.

We are looking for a lively and intelligent person to join our team as soon as possible.

The work will involve working in our London office, telephoning and corresponding with our overseas clients and agents, and some travel, mainly to European countries. Applicants should be fluent in at least one foreign language. Experience in marketing would be an asset but not essential.

The successful applicant will be paid top London rates and provided with generous removal expenses.

B Now listen to the three telephone messages and take notes. Each speaker is reporting on the interviews he or she has held in a different part of the country. You'll hear calls from:

Gus Morrison	Glasgow
Laura Steele	Sheffield
Terry Williams	Cardiff

Decide which of the job applicants sounds most promising. Which of them will you put on the short list for a second interview in London?

Compare your notes with the notes in the Key.

C Which of the three candidates do you rate most highly, judging from what you've heard about them?
If possible, compare your views with another student who has done this exercise.

13.7 Prepositional phrases – 3

Fill the gaps in these sentences with a suitable prepositional phrase from the list below. The first is done for you as an example.

on a large scale *on a ship/on a plane* *on approval*
on behalf of *on business* *on closer inspection*
on condition *on display* *on loan* *on order*
on paper *on request* *on schedule* *on the spot*
on the telephone *on time* *on vacation/on holiday*

1. They produce this kind of material on a large scale so they should be able to supply us quickly.
2. You will find our new product .... at our showroom.
3. We have a sales engineer .... who can fix the fault this week.
4. We can supply samples and demonstration equipment ....
5. We have had the goods .... for three months, but they haven't arrived yet.
6. We accepted delivery of the goods as undamaged, but .... we find that several of the components are unusable.
7. I spoke to him .... last week about this.
8. We can have the goods for four weeks .... Then we can return them or pay for them.
9. The goods arrived ....
10. We'll put the goods .... as soon as they're ready.
11. He travelled to England .... but managed to do a little sight-seeing while he was there.
12. I'm afraid Ms Smith is .... till the end of the month – can I help you?
13. We can offer you the job .... that you start work on the 1st of next month.

14. This candidate doesn't look very good .... but she is very impressive in person.
15. You can't keep this permanently, but you may have it .... till the end of the month.
16. She signed the letter .... her boss.
17. Our relocation plans are proceeding .... and we will be making the move on January 1 next year.

13.8 High-flyers

Listening

A Before you listen to the recording, look at this extract from a magazine article:

What is a high-flyer?

Many big companies today select their brightest and most capable young managers as "high-flyers". These are people who will be given special training and experience to make them into the top managers of tomorrow. It's a way of making sure that the company makes best use of its managers' potential. An ambitious young manager who is held back or stuck in a rut is likely to become restless and will start to look around to find a more challenging job elsewhere.

A typical high-flyer . . .

- is probably a man
- is under 40
- is in middle management
- is bright and ambitious
- has the 'right personality' to be a leader and an innovator
- does not need to have special knowledge or skills
- is someone who has been spotted early in his/her career and promoted early

---

B You'll hear part of a broadcast about high-flyers. Answer these multiple-choice questions about the information and opinions given in the recording.

According to Rod Scott:

1. In a large company . . .
   a) only a high-flyer can climb the promotion ladder more quickly.
   b) a bright person can quickly climb the promotion ladder even if there is no high-flyer scheme.
   c) the career structure is normally quite flexible.
2. High-flyer schemes are . . .
   a) found in all kinds of companies.
   b) most common in multi-national companies.
   c) common in large companies.

3. A member of a high-flyers scheme will...
   a) obtain wide experience in different departments.
   b) already have wide experience in different fields.
   c) become a specialist in his or her chosen field.
4. BP...
   a) is the world's largest multi-national company.
   b) has about 130,000 employees worldwide.
   c) has about 130,000 employees in the UK.
5. There are .... people participating in BP's 'individual development programme'.
   a) 130 b) 180 c) 260
6. BP's high-flyers join the scheme when...
   a) they have just joined the group.
   b) when they have been with the group for ten years.
   c) when they have already shown their potential.

According to Heather Stewart:

7. A high-flyer scheme may lead to...
   a) a management team who can work well together.
   b) a lack of flexibility in the management team.
   c) the business being prevented from changing.
8. A company with a high-flyer scheme tends...
   a) to be less competitive.
   b) not to recruit senior staff from outside the company.
   c) to lose good managers, who leave to join their competitors.
9. High-flyer schemes tend not to recognize the importance of...
   a) academic qualifications.
   b) people who join the company later.
   c) the experience and knowledge of older people.
10. Women managers are excluded from high-flyer schemes because...
    a) they are expected to leave to have babies.
    b) they prefer to have babies instead of a career.
    c) this is the age they are most likely to have babies.
11. Other able, enthusiastic managers...
    a) consider high-flyers to be better than them.
    b) lose their motivation.
    c) leave the company if they aren't selected as high-flyers.
12. In medium-size companies high-flyer schemes...
    a) are usually experimental.
    b) are unpopular.
    c) are unnecessary because the career structure is flexible.

14 Working together

14.1 Prepositional phrases – 4

Fill the gaps in these sentences with a suitable prepositional phrase.
The first one is done for you as an example.

of inferior quality	*out of date*	*to a certain extent*
of minor importance	*out of order*	*to the same effect*
of short duration	*out of stock*	*under separate cover*
through official channels	*out of work*	*under pressure*
through the usual channels		*with reference to*

1. We are sending you our Spring catalogue under separate cover.
2. You can get your raw materials ...., as long as you are prepared to pay the price asked.
3. Because the other items on the agenda were ...., the meeting was adjourned.
4. Although the works manager was .... from the director, he refused to change the working shifts.
5. If we can't solve the dispute ...., perhaps we should get someone in from outside.
6. It is at this stage of the process that any products .... are removed from the assembly line.
7. Even if the machines are ...., they should not be touched unless the power supply is off.
8. We informed them by phone of our decision, then sent them a letter ....
9. At a time when so many skilled workers are ...., it will be easy to fill the vacancy.
10. The old computers were really ....
11. .... your letter of 15 March, we are unable to offer you an alternative delivery date.
12. The strike was ...., so the production lost was minimal.
13. We'll have to reduce the workforce ...., perhaps by a process of voluntary redundancies.
14. We regret that we are unable to supply the items you ordered, as we are completely ....

14.2 Asking for and giving advice

First look at 14.1 in the Student's Book before you do this exercise.

A Which of these expressions can be used for

a) asking for advice from a friend
b) asking for advice from someone else
c) giving advice to a stranger
d) giving advice in a direct fashion
e) giving advice indirectly
f) accepting advice
g) rejecting advice

Mark the following expressions a, b, c etc. The first one is done for you as an example.

1. That's a good idea. ...
2. If I were in your position, I would...
3. Good idea, let's try that.
4. I should like to ask...
5. I would advise...
6. I'm not sure that's such a good idea.
7. I would appreciate your advice on...
8. Might it be an idea to...
9. Could I ask for some advice on...
10. Have you ever thought of...
11. I would recommend...
12. Well perhaps another time.
13. I'd like your advice on...
14. Why don't you...
15. Do you think I should...
16. No, I don't think I could do that.
17. My advice would be to...
18. You'd better...
19. What would you do if you were me?
20. If I were you I'd...
21. That sounds great, I'll try it.
22. What ought I to...

B You'll hear three short conversations. Answer these questions about each one:

1. How well do the people know each other?
2. What problem does each person have?
3. What advice does the other person give?
4. Does the person accept the advice given?

14.3 Vocabulary

Fill the gaps in these sentences and then add the words to the puzzle below:

1. You will receive a good salary plus fringe .... such as a company car.
2. Many companies keep .... files on their employees.
3. The .... was resolved when the management increased their offer.
4. As factories close, ... increases.
5. Production almost stopped completely during the ....
6. The company offers an attractive .... scheme for its employees.
7. If you want .... you'll have to do well in your progress interview.
8. We need a wage increase to .... our living standards.
9. The management threatened to .... the strike leaders.
10. The managing director announced a large number of .... because of the slump in orders from abroad.
11. The major .... to the firm's plans is the closure of two plants.
12. If they .... our demands, we will stay away from work.
13. Productivity has increased, since .... was introduced and employees can decide their working times.
14. Working on the night .... can be very unhealthy.
15. She can .... very skilfully on behalf of her members.
16. If the government .... on increasing tax, no one will work overtime.
17. .... is another expression for strike.

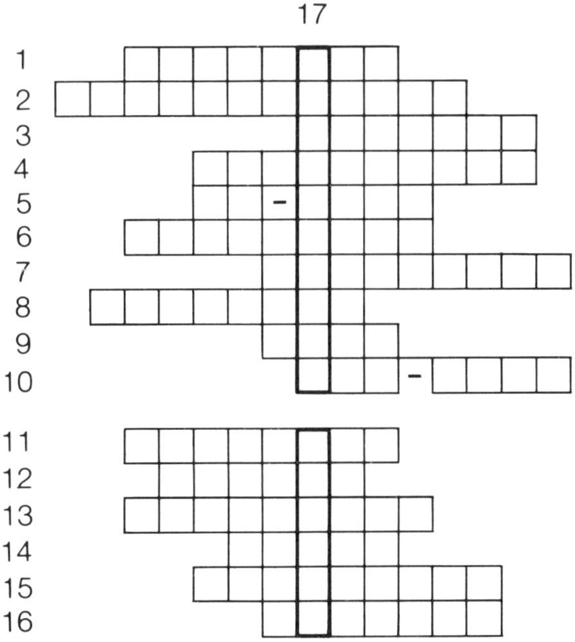

14.4 Order of adverbs

A Put the adverbs on the right of each sentence into the most 'comfortable' place in the sentence. The first one is done for you as an example.

1. *Fortunately* the company was able to increase its profits last year.	**fortunately**
2. European computer manufacturers are going to work together on this project.	**apparently**
3. The bonus was much higher than the management had planned.	**occasionally**
4. There has been a mistake made in this invoice.	**definitely**
5. If the management want the workforce to accept their offer, they must show more flexibility.	**sincerely**
6. We asked to see the union representatives before we made the decision.	**specifically**
7. The customer was quite satisfied with our after-sales service.	**initially**
8. The order book is stagnating.	**currently**
9. Although the freight was handled, important components were broken in transit.	**carefully**
10. We have increased our product range in order to give our customers more choice.	**gradually**

B Put the adverbs on the right in the correct position in each sentence.

1. We are going to investigate the whole question as soon as possible.	**certainly**
2. In a different economic climate the workforce would have accepted the pay deal.	**probably**
3. The customers complain when we send John instead of Margaret to the sales conference.	**always**
4. The managing director writes in the internal newsletter about the progress the company is making.	**often**
5. The supervisor is able to find somebody who is willing to stay behind to take the late overseas orders.	**never**
6. The designers have completed the new company logo.	**nearly**
7. If the correct procedure is followed, you will have a breakdown.	**hardly ever**
8. Our head office forgot to appoint an overseas agent for European sales.	**almost**
9. The management has announced the plan for rationalizing production on this site.	**just**
10. Do you think the firm will get the Chinese order?	**ever**

14.5 Company training

Listening

A Look at this paragraph from a magazine:

Gurus and motivated trainers are in great demand among US corporations as changing market conditions mean that they have to think about increasing their productivity. And what is more some companies are prepared to pay these New Age gurus big money to change their employees' frame of mind.

B You're going to hear a radio programme on the subject of special training in American companies. As you listen to the radio programme for the first time try and answer these questions:

1. Why are companies using these training programmes?
2. Why are they popular with some companies?
3. Who are the critics of these programmes?

C Now listen to the recording once more and answer these specific questions:

4. What New Age training programme names are mentioned?
5. What is meant by the New Age system?
6. How do some workers describe the programmes?
7. How many of its employees is an American telephone company sending on special seminars?
8. What techniques do almost all of the programmes place great emphasis on?
9. Which of these items are *not* one of the 'six essentials of organizational health':

freedom	duration	concentration	rationality
security	identity	order	resources
position	relation	interaction	expansion

10. The employees are expected to say that their own behaviour is the result of...
    a) external stimuli (i.e. stimuli from outside)
    b) themselves
    c) a 'purpose that is beyond themselves'
11. What criticisms do people have of the training?
12. What does one of the supporters of such schemes say that companies need to develop?
13. Why are no companies going to admit to failure especially if the results are not visible?

14.6 Unions and technological change

Writing

Read this letter from the General Secretary of a banking union writing to his members in the union newsletter.

A There are a few improvements which could be made to the letter. There are also several punctuation errors (especially misplaced commas) which need correcting.

Rewrite this letter and then compare your letter with the model letter in the key.

Dear Colleague,

In the year 1983 our union's national banking committee published a booklet "After 1984", which outlined the systems, which many large banks had already introduced or planned to introduce in the near future.

During that time, many people said our predictions were stupid and that we were exaggerating. We only wish we had been.

The banks have proceeded rapidly with the introduction of technology, without demonstrating an awareness of the need to reach agreement on the effects on employment, career structure, promotion prospects or the many other aspects of working life, which technology influences.

Our union is aware of the advantages and dangers of new technology; we accept that technological development will bring about changes in our industry, but we cannot accept, that this change will be at the expense of our members' jobs and career prospects.

It is for this reason that we have been seeking a 'New Technology Agreement' in order that changes in the banks can be introduced on a bilateral, rather than a unilateral basis.

I ask you to give your full support to our campaign and to help to explain to non-members, how vital it is for them to join our union. In this way we can achieve protection for your future through agreements negotiated by a strong and independent union.

Technology can bring uncertainty and a worsening of conditions and an improvement through a shorter working week, more employment opportunities and greater job satisfaction. The choice is yours - with us.

Yours sincerely

Frank Kelly
General Secretary

B Answer these questions.

1. According to the text the union ...
   a) criticized the banks' systems
   b) introduced the banks' systems
   c) summarized the banks' systems

2. The union ...
   a) predicted that the systems would be stupid
   b) wished it had got its predictions right
   c) wished it had been exaggerating

3. According to the text the banks ...
   a) have proceeded with the introduction of technology
   b) have not demonstrated the need for technology
   c) are trying to reach agreement with the union

4. The union ...
   a) accepts technological development
   b) considers that technological development is a threat
   c) believes technological change is too expensive

5. According to the text the union needs to ...
   a) explain its position to the banks
   b) protect the agreements it has already made
   c) reach agreement on new developments

15 Revision

The exercises in this unit revise the skills and language points that you've covered in *International Business English*. These exercises are not directly connected with the theme of Unit 15 in the Student's Book.

Your teacher may wish you to use some of these exercises as a progress test. In this case, please don't use the Answer Key while you're doing the exercises.

15.1 Grammar revision

Decide how best to fill the gap in each of these sentences, as in this example:

How many copies .... with the order?
a) did we sent
b) sent we
c) have we sended
d) did we send ✓

1. I remember asking him on the phone last November ....
   a) that the goods arrived on time.
   b) when the goods will arrive.
   c) if the goods would arrive on time.
   d) whether the goods arrived on time.

2. I can't find my glasses. .... them anywhere in the office this morning?
   a) Did you see c) Have you seen
   b) Saw you d) Did you have

3. Their product .... more imaginatively this season.
   a) is being marketed c) is been marketed
   b) is marketing d) is marketed

4. If we want to make a big impact, ... consider a TV campaign.
   a) we'll have to b) we better c) we had to d) we've got

5. A word processor is .... a typewriter.
   a) more easier to use than c) as easy to use as
   b) easier to use as d) not as easy to use than

6. If you .... ice in warm water, it soon melts.
   a) will place   b) would place   c) place   d) placed

7. The level of discount .... the size of the order that is placed.
   a) is depending of   c) is depending on
   b) depends of   d) depends on

8. We are looking forward .... you at next year's conference.
   a) to see   b) to seeing   c) seeing   d) that we will see

9. The warehouse entrance is .... the main car park.
   a) opposite to   c) opposite from
   b) opposite of   d) opposite

10. The new price lists .... tomorrow and will be available in a few days.
   a) are being printed   c) were printed
   b) are printed   d) will print

11. He told us that he .... for a new job.
   a) thought he would apply   c) is applying
   b) applied   d) had been applying

12. If the components .... delivered earlier we might have been able to start work on time.
   a) might have been   c) would have been
   b) were   d) had been

13. When .... writing the report of the meeting?
   a) have you finished   c) do you finish
   b) are you finishing   d) will you have finished

14. Mr Brown .... ten years.
   a) has been head of this department for
   b) is head of this department for
   c) is head of this department since
   d) has been head of this department since

15. The number of orders went up .... we increased our prices by 15%.
   a) because   b) although   c) when   d) if

16. Mr Black is the .... office you'll be sharing this month.
   a) man, whose   c) man of whom the
   b) man, of whom the   d) man whose

17. These documents arrived on Thursday, ...
   a) arrived they?   c) didn't they?
   b) didn't there?   d) weren't they?

18. .... our new brochure, which should arrive next week.
   a) I just have sent   c) just I have sent
   b) I have just sent   d) I have sent just

19. When the post ...., I'll bring it in to your office.
   a) will arrive c) is arriving
   b) arrives d) is going to arrive

20. .... an English course can be an interesting experience.
   a) To assist c) Attending
   b) To attend d) Assisting

15.2 Word-building revision

Fill the gaps in these sentences with a word built from the word given on the right. Here is an example:

BP is a large ...multinational... corporation.	**nation**
1. Before operating the machine, you must .... the screws.	**tight**
2. You'll be impressed by the .... of this equipment.	**flexible**
3. The .... of their offices has cost a lot of money.	**modern**
4. The applicant is too .... for us to consider employing him.	**experience**
5. To say that exporting is profitable is an	**simple**
6. We've had complaints because the machine is	**rely**
7. We're still waiting for the .... of the loan we gave them.	**pay**
8. Turn the handle .... to open the door.	**clock**
9. She is a very good manager and	**administrate**
10. Thank you for your .... , it was very helpful.	**recommend**

15.3 Prepositions revision

Fill the gaps in these sentences with the right prepositions, as in this example:

We must give priority ....to.......... export orders.

1. There is a lack .... information .... that company.
2. We still have 200 boxes .... order .... you.
3. The consignment consists .... four large crates .... all.
4. Max was left .... charge .... the department for too long.
5. He signed the documents .... behalf .... his company.
6. She retired .... the firm .... the age of sixty.
7. .... reference .... your order, we apologize for the delay.
8. We always insist .... payment .... advance.
9. Can you deal .... this report in time .... the meeting?
10. I've never visited Britain .... business, only .... holiday.

15.4 Vocabulary revision

Here, for a change, is a complete crossword puzzle:

CLUES ACROSS

1. Put down these arrangements to meet people in your diary
7. Payment in instalments
9. Money to start a business
10. When several people run a firm and share the profits each is a ....
11. Stamp dealers pay more for a stamp if it is ....
12. Requests for goods
15. How many millions are there in a billion?
17. A project for the future
20. A computer program is ....ware
21. Employees receive these when they retire
23. A customer gets one as proof of payment
24. Against the law
27. Every boss has one to deal with correspondence
29. A self-employed business person has his or her .... business
30. Puts his or her name at the end of a letter
31. These supply the raw material for paper
32. Abbreviation for Street

CLUES DOWN

1. Open one at a bank
2. Money is printed on this
3. The extra you pay the bank for a loan
4. Another word for 'until'
5. Opposite of import
6. A sales figure you aim to achieve
8. This department deals with recruitment and staffing
13. This department deals with selling
14. Money put into a business in the hope of making a profit
16. Where business people spend most of their working hours
18. A prediction of what something will cost
19. 'A .... and his money are soon parted.'
20. Stoppages of work due to industrial disputes
22. An unusual business which employs clowns and animals!
25. A business supplies its clients with either .... or services
26. Opposite of borrow
28. When shareholders accept a take-over bid, they are saying '............'

(Thanks very much to David and Rosemary Brown for this crossword puzzle!)

15.5 Functions revision

This exercise revises some of the functions you have practised.

A Look at the expressions below. Which of them would you use to express each of these ideas?

What would you say . . .

a) if you do not want to accept the advice someone is giving you?
b) when you want to complain indirectly to someone?
c) when you want to tell someone a story?
d) if you've not understood an explanation?
e) when you wish to agree with someone?
f) if you want to interrupt someone in a discussion to say something?
g) when it's unlikely that you can do something?
h) when you would like a person to do something for you?
i) when you want to give someone some information?
j) when someone you already know is introduced to you?

Expressions

1. Did I ever tell you about . . ?
2. Yes, I'm all in favour of that . . .
3. I doubt if we'll be able to . . .
4. I think you should know that . . .
5. I'm not sure that's such a good idea.
6. Yes, I think we've met before. Good to see you again.
7. There may have been a misunderstanding about . . .
8. Could I make a suggestion?
9. Do you think you could . . .?
10. I'm sorry, what did you say . . .

B Listen to the cassette. You'll first hear a telephone conversation and then three short conversations. Set the counter to zero before you play each conversation, so that you can easily find the beginning again. Which of these headings describe what the people are doing in the conversations? Put ticks (√) beside the functions.

Conversation	1	2	3	4
a) asking permission to do something				
b) requesting				
c) offering to help				
d) agreeing or disagreeing				
e) asking for or giving information				
f) complaining				
g) apologizing				
h) telling a story				

Conversation	1	2	3	4
i) explaining or giving instructions j) asking for and giving advice				

C Now listen to the conversations again. Decide which of these statements are true or false.

1. a) Francis Lissetzky is not satisfied with the replacement for the M49 electric motor.
   b) Anita Lichtenstein says the testing engineers will work day and night to get it ready.
   c) Francis Lissetzky discovered the problem a week ago.
   d) Francis Lissetzky says they require the machine to run the pumps.
   e) Anita Lichtenstein thinks that certain programmes should not be run.

2. a) The salesperson believes in her product.
   b) The customer is more interested in the price than what the product looks like.
   c) The salesperson is not sure whether they can give a discount.

3. a) The customer is interested in the XL 130 model.
   b) The customer says the batteries are fitted in last.
   c) The salesperson sticks a piece of plastic on the back of the model.
   d) The salesperson tells the customer how long the working life of the batteries is.

4. a) The salesman considers the model to be the best on the market.
   b) The customer takes pictures himself in artificial lighting.
   c) The customer thinks it is necessary to use the right lens.
   d) The salesman is not sure what one ought to tell ordinary photographers.

D Write down what you would say in these situations. Here is an example:

The receptionist tells you on the intercom that Mr Martin has arrived.
Oh good, could you ask him to come up, please?

1. Mr Martin, a client, has arrived on his annual visit to your office.
2. He asks if he can make a long distance phone call after your meeting.
3. A plane flying over makes it impossible for you to hear the reason he gives.
4. He says his Christmas order didn't arrive till mid-January. You know this, but blame the shipping department.
5. He says that he called the shipping manager, but just got a rude, unhelpful reply. Thank him for this information.
6. Your new product will sell well – make sure he knows this.
7. He says your new product is just right for his market. You agree.
8. He asks you to show him how your new product works. How do you begin your explanation?

⇛

9. He wonders if he should place an order for 200 or 250 units.
10. You have just remembered an amusing experience. How do you begin telling Mr Martin the story?

Note:
Your teacher has special role play material in the Teacher's Book, which can be photocopied and used as part of an oral progress test.

15.6 Midway International *Writing*

The situation:
You work for Midway International, a trading company in your own country. One of your suppliers is Original Products plc in Scotland, who manufacture a range of high-tech products. One of your customers is Ultimate Pty in Australia.
Your company has received the letter on the next page. Your boss, Mr Meyer, has told you to take appropriate action and he has left you some notes (see Guiding points below).

Write two letters or faxes:
A to Original Products plc, B to Ultimate Pty.
You are on first-name terms with Bruce Dundee of Ultimate, but not with Mrs McArthur of Original Products.

GUIDING POINTS (Make sure you deal with all these points in your letters)

A Guiding points for letter or fax to Mrs McArthur

1. Hurry up or we will cancel order – we must receive the units by 1 May.
2. Make sure we have priority over other customers.
3. Speed of the unit is *considerably* slower than specification – Our customers may not find this acceptable and price should be $45 lower.
4. re feedback on OP 424 series: we'll ask our own customers for comments.
5. We have one OP 424 in our head office: seems to overheat, but hasn't broken down – yet!
6. In case of breakdown, should users return defective units to your factory?

B Guiding points for letter or fax to Mr Bruce Dundee, Ultimate Pty, 4130 Pacific Drive, Brisbane, Australia.

1. Apologize for delay in supplying order UP/901 for 10 OP 232s.
2. Explain reasons for delay.
3. We plan to ship to you on 2 May by air freight – or earlier if possible.
4. Mention our worries about speed reduction – will this affect you?
5. Manufacturer may reduce price – we'll pass this saving on to you.
6. Ask for feedback on OP 424 series.
7. Ask if any OP 424s have broken down.
8. Send greetings to Sheila (Bruce's wife).

ORIGINAL PRODUCTS plc

20 KIRKTON CAMPUS LIVINGSTON EH54 6QA SCOTLAND

Midway International
P.O. Box 777
K-4550 Euroville
Yourland

April 2, 19--

Dear Mr Meyer,

Your order: MI/876

We regret to inform you that there will be a delay in delivery of your order number MI/876 for 200 of our OP 232s. This is due to a number of problems we have been having with CPUs. We found that we were having to reject an unacceptable proportion of these and it has been necessary for us to look further afield for an alternative supply. However, we have today secured the firm promise of a supply of US-manufactured 68020s, which we expect to receive by airfreight within the month.

As a result of using the 68020 instead of the original 68000, the processing speed of the unit is now slightly reduced from 12.0 MHz to 9.7 MHz. This should represent no compatibility problems for users.

May I take this opportunity of asking you for some feedback on our OP 424 series products? We are keen to have information on your own and your customers' reactions to the price, packaging and design of these units. Also, if you have any comments on the performance and reliability of these units, perhaps you could let me know as we have been getting some unconfirmed reports of failures.

Thank you very much for your help and patience.

Let me assure you that we will make our best efforts to expedite your order.

Yours sincerely,

Janet McArthur

J. McArthur (Mrs)

TELEPHONE: 44 506 444777 TELEX: 727871 FACSIMILE: 44 506 33881

15.7 The Peterborough Effect – 1

Reading

There are 20 reading comprehension questions altogether in exercises 15.7 to 15.9.

Read the text carefully, then choose the correct answers to the questions below.

1. Before they acquired the 20-acre site, Pearl Group...
   a) already had one site in Peterborough.
   b) already had two sites in Peterborough.
   c) had no sites in Peterborough.
2. Pearl plan to relocate to Peterborough so that...
   a) they can redevelop their London head office.
   b) they can operate efficiently and keep costs low.
   c) their products will be more competitive.
3. Staff will start moving to Peterborough...
   a) shortly before the new building is completed.
   b) when the new building is completed.
   c) long before the new building is completed.
4. When the new building is complete, Pearl's Thorpe Wood building will...
   a) be used as temporary offices.
   b) not be used by Pearl.
   c) be used as its computer centre.
5. The new building in Peterborough Business Park will house Pearl's
   a) headquarters.
   b) headquarters and five regional offices.
   c) headquarters, computer and accounts centre, and five regional offices.
6. Moving to Peterborough will save Pearl...
   a) £1 million a year. b) £2 million a year. c) £3 million a year.
7. Peterborough was chosen, rather than another location, because of
   a) Pearl's successful relocation of its computer and accounts centre.
   b) Peterborough's closeness to London.
   c) Thomas Cook's successful relocation to Peterborough.
8. The total number of Pearl employees in Peterborough will be...
   a) 200 to 300. b) 1600. c) 2000.
9. When Pearl's new building is complete...
   a) 1600 employees will move to the new offices.
   b) 400 employees will move to the new offices.
   c) 1600 employees can move to the new offices if they wish.
10. Pearl Group's business is...
    a) manufacturing. b) life assurance. c) travel services.

the Peterborough Effect

PEARL RELOCATES

The Pearl Group is to relocate its London headquarters and five regional offices to Peterborough in a move involving 2,000 jobs.

Pearl has obtained a 20-acre site at Peterborough Business Park, on which it will develop a 250,000 square feet building at a cost of £25 million.

Construction is planned to start in Spring 1988, with the new building ready for occupation in 1991. In the meantime, Pearl will start moving staff into temporary accommodation in Peterborough later this year.

It is the second major endorsement of Peterborough by the Pearl Group.

In 1973, Pearl Assurance obtained a 10-acre site from the Development Corporation at Thorpe Wood for its computer and accounts centre.

The 400 staff who currently work at Thorpe Wood will transfer to the new offices and the older building, says Pearl, "will be surplus to requirements and will be further developed as an investment".

A further 1,600 staff employed by the Group will be given the opportunity to move to Peterborough. Pearl estimates that its relocation decision will create an annual demand of between 200 and 300 jobs in the Peterborough area.

Group Chairman Einion Holland said: "To maintain its position as one of the UK's leading life offices, Pearl must be able to offer its customers the products they want at the right price.

"This requires the combination of operational flexibility and efficiency and low costs, which it would have been impossible to achieve at our existing Chief Office.

"The ability to centralise our operations in Peterborough and to develop the most up to date computer systems which only a purpose-designed building will allow, will bring important long term benefits for our customers, shareholders and employees".

Pearl has occupied the same High Holborn building since 1915. Now the entire building is in need of major refurbishment, but no decision has yet been made about its development.

It is estimated that among the long term savings created by the move to Peterborough will be running costs of £1 million a year, and London weighting of £2 million.

Peterborough beat off competition from other places because of Pearl's experience of the successful 1973 relocation, and because of the quality of the site at the business park.

For Peterborough, it is the biggest single relocation out of more than 420 firms attracted since the city's expansion programme began in 1970, beating the move of travel organisation Thomas Cook from London to Thorpe Wood which involved more than 1,000 jobs.

Development Corporation General Manager Kenneth Hutton said: "This is the best news we have had. We have been working on this project for many months, and we knew that Pearl was looking at several other places very seriously. Peterborough won because it was the best".

15.8 The Peterborough Effect – 2 *Reading*

Read the text carefully, then choose the correct answers to the questions below.

Americans choose city as a pivot for European trade

Chesterton World Manager Steve Chapman *(left)* and Development Corporation Chairman Jeremy Rowe are shown computer communications equipment by Annalise Cowley, Manager of the new centre.

An American firm which uses the most sophisticated communications equipment has chosen Peterborough as the pivot between its European customers and manufacturing plants around the world.

Chesterton (UK) Ltd is part of Chesterton International, a specialist engineering group based in Massachusetts.

Its new European Customer Service Centre has been set up in offices in a converted older building on the edge of Peterborough's Queensgate covered shopping centre.

The new centre will receive orders from all parts of Europe, translate them, and pass them to the Chesterton factories in Holland, Eire and the USA.

Each of its Peterborough staff has mastery of at least one European language – and all but one of them were recruited from the locality.

Chesterton specialises in pumps and sealing devices used in the process industries. International Manager Philip Metz said: "Peterborough was chosen because it was the place which best met our criteria of central location, high technology communications capability and the availability of highly educated quality staff".

The Peterborough operation is a return 'home' for the company, which was formed 102 years ago by A. W. Chesterton soon after emigrating to America from the East Midlands town of Loughborough.

1. Chesterton's Peterborough offices are...
   a) purpose-built.
   b) near the shopping centre.
   c) extremely attractive.

2. The new centre will receive orders...
   a) from European countries.
   b) from all over the world.
   c) from the United States.

3. The new centre is being set up because...
   a) it is expensive for customers to communicate with the USA direct.
   b) orders are placed in many different languages.
   c) Chesterton has so many factories in Europe.

4. Every member of the new centre's staff can speak English and...
   a) one or more European languages.
   b) more than one European language.
   c) one European language.

5. The new centre's staff...
   a) all come from Peterborough.
   b) mostly come from the Peterborough area.
   c) all come from the Peterborough area.

6. Chesterton's business is...
   a) communications.
   b) processing.
   c) manufacturing.

7. Peterborough was chosen because of its location and because...
   a) the founder of the company came from the East Midlands.
   b) Chesterton has no factories in the UK.
   c) suitable staff were available.

15.9 The Nightingale Effect

Reading and reading aloud

A READING

Read the text and then tick (√) the correct statements opposite ⟶

B READING ALOUD

1. Read the text aloud and record your reading on a blank cassette.
2. Compare your reading with the model reading on the self-study cassette.

If you've discovered the Peterborough effect we think you'll appreciate the Nightingale effect

Moving out of town has many advantages, but it does leave your business with one inevitable problem . . . where to hold those meetings that simply have to be in London.

Nightingale has solved the problem. The Nightingale Business Identity Plan provides your company with all year round London representation at a fraction of the cost of a full time London office.

Immediately you'll have access to some of the smartest offices in Mayfair's Berkeley Square, equipped with the latest communications technology and staffed by real professionals.

Incoming calls will be answered personally and your mail handled and dealt with while you're away. And when you're in town your meetings will run like clockwork.

Telephone or write to Linda Godfriaux-Wilson now for full details of The Nightingale Business Identity Plan.

NIGHTINGALE
SECRETARIAT

NO3 BERKELEY SQUARE
London WIX 5HG. Telephone (01) 629 6116.
Telex 267383 ANEWHOG. Fax (01) 491 4811.
A member of The Leading Business Centres of The World.

1. Nightingale's business is . . .
   a) communications.
   b) organizing meetings.
   c) office and secretarial services.
2. If you have relocated to Peterborough . . .
   a) meetings in London are no longer necessary.
   b) some meetings must still be held in London.
   c) you'll still want to impress clients with a smart London office.
3. Nightingale has offices . . .
   a) in the best address in London.
   b) all over London.
   c) all over the world.

15.10 Franchising

Listening

You'll hear a recording of part of a training session for small businessmen or women on the principles and practice of franchising.

A Before you listen to the recording, read this introductory text:

Franchising

The principle of franchising is that the **franchisor** sells an established, successful business format to a **franchisee**, who will carry on the business in a clearly defined territory.

All franchises trade under the same name and appear to be branches of one large firm, not independent companies. In the USA, most of the well-known fast food restaurant chains and hotel/motel chains are actually franchises. Some examples are: McDonald's restaurants, Budget Rent-A-Car and Tandy/Radio Shack stores.

B Now listen to the first part of the recording. Fill the gaps in this summary.

The franchisor usually supplies:

1. an .... product or service and a well-known .... image
2. a .... manual, showing how the business should be set up and how it must be run
3. help, advice and training in .... the business
4. continuing advice, training and support during the .... of franchise
5. the .... that's required to set up and operate the business
6. .... of the product, which he will be able to .... cheaply in .... This may result in savings or, depending on franchisor's mark-up, ... the franchisee to buying at .... the market price.
7. local, national and even international ....

C Now listen to the rest of the recording and answer these questions about it:

1. The questioner points out that . . .
   a) franchisees usually require varying amounts of on-going support.
   b) franchisors tend to reduce their on-going support a year after start-up.
   c) not all franchisors give the same quality of support.
2. She also points out that, as a franchisee, you must find out . . .
   a) what brand image and support the franchisor is providing.
   b) what level of help you will be getting after a year or so.
   c) what level of help you will get when you start up the franchise.
3. In the case of problems in running the franchise, you need to know:
   a) Will the franchisor be able to solve all your problems?
   b) Will the franchisor provide financial support in an emergency?
   c) Will you be offered regular advice by the franchisor?
4. In his answer, the lecturer points out that the franchisee should find out what help he'll get from the franchisor . . .
   a) in recruiting staff.
   b) in training his/her present staff in new skills.
   c) in training new staff.
5. You should also find out whether . . .
   a) the franchisor will continue to research and develop the product.
   b) the product has been thoroughly researched and developed.
   c) the franchisor will charge you a levy for R & D.
6. You need to know whether the franchisor is . . .
   a) continuing to advertise the product.
   b) spending as much on advertising as the franchisees are charged.
   c) spending enough money on advertising.
7. The lecturer goes on to say that a franchisee pays the franchisor . . .
   a) a substantial capital sum
   b) a monthly fee
   c) both a capital sum and a monthly fee
8. To raise money to pay for a franchise, a franchisee . . .
   a) will probably have a lot of difficulty in getting a bank loan.
   b) will probably have little difficulty in getting a bank loan.
   c) must have an enormous amount of money in the bank.
9. The franchisor's income from a franchise is calculated on the basis of . . .
   a) the franchisee's net profits.
   b) the franchisee's total sales.
   c) the franchisee's monthly income from the franchise.
10. If a franchisee wants to sell the franchise to someone else . . .
    a) he must have the franchisor's permission.
    b) he must pay the franchisor a substantial commission.
    c) he is not allowed to do this. He must sell it back to the franchisor.

15.11 Finally . . .

Dear Reader,

Congratulations on finishing the exercises in the Workbook !
We hope you've enjoyed using 'International Business English' as much as we've enjoyed writing it !

Goodbye and best wishes,

Leo Jones   Richard Alexander

Answer key

1 Face to face

1.1 Asking questions

A

3. How long have you been working here?
4. Which room do you keep your sales files in?
5. Why do you never phone in the morning?
6. When did you start working for the firm?
7. What kind of room would you like?
8. Who did you hear about this product from?
9. How much does the complete package cost?
10. How many copies of the company report did they print?

B

3. ..., won't they?
4. ..., can't we?
5. ..., can they?
6. ..., is she?
7. ..., does it?
8. ..., don't you?
9. ..., haven't you?
10. ..., should we?

C

3. They'll let us know before the end of the month – that's right, isn't it?
4. Am I right in saying that we can send the catalogues by surface mail?
5. I don't think that they can provide us with the information we need.
6. Is it true that she isn't in the office today?
7. As far as I know, this machine doesn't operate automatically.
8. I think you know a great deal about economics.
9. I expect you've studied this subject for some time.
10. I don't think we should interrupt the meeting.

1.2 Have you met ... ?

B WHAT WOULD YOU SAY?

Suggested answers (many variations are possible):

2. Hello, Tony. Nice to meet you.
3. That's right, yes, we once worked together in ...
4. I'm terribly sorry, I've forgotten your name.
5. Yes, good morning, my name's ... I've got an appointment with ...
6. Did you have a good journey? It's very nice of you to come all this way.
7. Would you like a coffee? *or* Would you like something to drink?
8. Good heavens, is that the time. I didn't realize it was so late. I really must be going now.

1.3 Around the world

A

8

1 Egyptian
2 French
3 Belgian
4 Brazilian
5 Swiss
6 Austrian
7 Danish

16

9 Bulgarian
10 Greek
11 Italian
12 Dutch
13 Swedish
14 Portuguese
15 Turkish

B

1 Iran
2 New Zealand
3 Denmark
4 Indonesia
5 Algeria

6 The Philippines
7 Argentina
8 Kenya
9 Ireland
10 Syria
11 Turkey
12 Australia
13 Nigeria

2 Letters, telexes and memos

2.1 Spelling and punctuation mistakes

The 13 spelling mistakes are corrected below:

Madam	quite	discount
information	available	received
catalogue	enclosed	products
compatible	further	pieces
which		

The 13 punctuation mistakes have been corrected here:

I AM AFRAID THAT WE HAVE NOT BEEN ABLE TO CONTACT YOU BY TELEPHONE. MY SECRETARY CALLED THROUGHOUT THE DAY YESTERDAY AT HALF-HOURLY INTERVALS BUT WAS TOLD THAT YOU WERE "NOT AVAILABLE". PLEASE CONTACT ME PERSONALLY AS SOON AS POSSIBLE BECAUSE WE NEED TO CHECK A NUMBER OF DETAILS IN YOUR ORDER.
YOU CAN REACH ME BY TELEPHONE AT ANY TIME THIS AFTERNOON OR TOMORROW MORNING. OUR OFFICE HOURS ARE 8.30 TO 5. YOU CAN LEAVE A MESSAGE FOR ME TO CALL YOU BACK IF NECESSARY.

2.2 Vocabulary

15

1 clear
2 enclose
3 esquire
4 reference
5 zip code
6 post code
7 p.p.
8 acknowledge
9 columns
10 word processors
11 style
12 memorandum
13 catalog
14 catalogue

2.3 Should we send them a fax or a telex?

04 HOW MUCH DO THEY COST!

■ A good basic fax machine will cost around £2000. But you could pay up to around £8000.

05 WHAT DOES IT COST TO LEASE A FAX MACHINE?

■ Between £150 and £500 per quarter, depending on the complexity of the machine.

06 ARE FACSIMILES AS GOOD AS THE ORIGINALS?

■ The reproduction is very good although not absolutely perfect to the trained eye. You optimise the results by choosing the most appropriate machine for your kind of work: 'line machines' are excellent for handwriting, type and line drawings, while 'half-tone machines' can reproduce illustrations and photographic material, as efficiently as a good photocopier. The quality can be improved by using 'fine mode'.

ORIGINAL LINE

FAXED LINE

07 CAN I BE SURE THAT THE FACSIMILE IS CORRECT?

■ You can check to see that your own fax machine is making a fair copy by using it in just the same way as a photocopier. Assuming it is, and that there is no interference, the facsimile will be transmitted exactly.

08 WHAT DOES IT COST TO SEND A FAX?

■ The rates are exactly the same as for telephone calls. Currently it would cost about 6p to send one A4 page before noon within a 34 mile radius (the British Telecom standard for a local call). You can work out the cost of sending a fax abroad by consulting the latest British Telecom International Direct Dialling (IDD) charges leaflet.

09 CAN I TAKE ADVANTAGE OF CHEAP RATES?

■ Yes. Some fax machines have a 'delayed send' facility. In other words, you can choose the time when the document is sent (during the cheap rate period, for example), preset that time, and leave the machine to transmit automatically.

10 HOW DO I KNOW IF MY MESSAGE HAS GOT THROUGH?

■ Good machines automatically stamp the original as soon as it has been transmitted and produce a receipt as soon as the facsimile reaches its destination.

11 HOW CAN I KEEP TRACK OF MY FAX TRAFFIC?

■ Most machines automatically print out a log showing the date, the time and the customer's identity. You can keep these records on file.

12 DOES A FAX TAKE UP MUCH SPACE?

■ No. The current machines are roughly the same size and weight as an office typewriter, some are even smaller.

13 ARE THEY NOISY?

■ They vary, but generally no noisier in use than an electric typewriter.

14 DOES A FAX NEED A TRAINED OPERATOR?

■ No. Anyone can use a fax machine. It is as simple as making a photocopy and a telephone call.

15 IS A FACSIMILE A LEGAL DOCUMENT?

■ Strictly speaking, no.

2.4 Make a good impression

This improved version of Mr Burke's letter shows just one way the letter could be written – many variations are possible:

Dear Mr Brown,

Thank you very much for your letter and your order.

Unfortunately, in common with other suppliers, our prices have risen since you placed an order with us two years ago, but you will be pleased to hear that we will supply your current order at the old price.

I enclose our new catalogue and price lists, which contain several exciting new products and our latest prices.

I will keep you fully informed about the progress of your order. If you would like to get in touch with me urgently, our new fax number is 998321 or, of course, you may prefer to phone or telex me as before.

Yours sincerely,

A. Burke

Sales Director

2.5 Can you tell me how to spell that?

The correct spellings are given on the cassette:

In the odd-numbered sentences, the second spelling is correct.
In the even-numbered sentences, the first spelling is correct.

Make sure you can spell the words out loud, easily and fluently, and not just write them correctly.

2.6 Joining sentences

A

2. If you send us another copy of your invoice, we will pay it at once.
3. Before the consignment was loaded on to the truck, it was packed for export.
4. While each order is manufactured, the packaging is printed.
5. Because your letter was delayed in the post, we have not been able to process your order yet.
6. So that we can reply to your query at once, please inform us of your telex number.

B

2. The package was so heavy that a single man couldn't lift it.
3. Although the order arrived late, we were able to supply the goods on time.
4. In spite of fog at the airport, our plane landed safely.
5. Because of a mistake in the hotel booking, I had to find another hotel.
6. In order to avoid any mistakes, I sent a telex.

C

2. Because your letter to us and our letter to you were both posted yesterday, the letters crossed in the post.
3. Our company has a long tradition but our letters look old-fashioned and, as we are trying to modernize the company's image, all our correspondence should be word-processed.
4. Because short sentences are both easy to write and understand and long words can be confusing, a simple style of writing letters is recommended.

2.7 Improve these letters

A

with 13 spelling and punctuation mistakes underlined:

I noticed your advertisment in the Daily Planet amd I would be gratefull if you could sned me further information about your products My company is considering subcontracting some of its office services and I beleive that you may be able ot supply us with a sutiable service, Looking forware to hearing form you. Yours faithfully.

A

with mistakes corrected:

I noticed your advertisment in the Daily Planet and I would be grateful if you could send further information about your products.

My company is considering subcontracting some of its office services and I believe that you may be able to supply us with a suitable service.

Looking forward to hearing from you,

Yours faithfully,

B

with improved layout and paragraphs:

Thank you very much for your letter of 15 January, which we received today.

In answer to your enquiry we have pleasure in enclosing an information pack, giving full details of our services.

If you would like any further information, do please contact me by phone or in writing and I will be pleased to help.

I hope that our services will be of interest to you and I look forward to hearing from you.

Yours sincerely,

C

with shorter, clearer sentences:

There are a number of queries that I would like to raise about your products. I would be grateful if you could ask a representative to get in touch with me so that I can discuss these queries. Hopefully, I will be able to place an order if the queries are satisfactorily answered.

3 On the phone

3.1 Misunderstandings on the phone

PART ONE

'Can you send us 300 kilos of white rice at 18 cents per kilo?'
'We require 2 boxes of ripe bananas.'
'The price per case is £115.'
'So the total price is 4,295 francs.'
'Our phone number is 456982.'

PART TWO

1. position
2. right person
3. guess
4. brief
5. bad line call back
6. friendly
7. Smile
8. technical abbreviations
9. figures names quantities
10. numbers
11. interrupt
12. lunch hour
13. information

3.2 Vocabulary

1. speaking
2. hold
3. intercom
4. extension
5. message
6. calling
7. dialled
8. ring
9. diary
10. assistance

11 (down): phonecards

3.3 What would you write?

Suggested answers (many variations are possible):

1. Could you please telephone me about this next week?
2. Would you mind confirming this by telex?
3. I regret to say that we are unable to offer you a special discount.
4. Please let us know if you would like us to send you a sample of this product.
5. With your permission, we propose to ship the order in two separate consignments.
6. Thank you very much for your kind assistance.
7. If you have any questions about our literature, do please let me know.
8. Unfortunately, we are unable to make amendments to an order by telephone.

3.7 Present tenses

A

2. picks up
3. deserve
4. is assisting
5. is looking up
6. am attending
7. prints out
8. get through
9. am putting you through
10. am making

B

2. we aren't making it up this week.
3. it doesn't print out the figures every day.
4. I'm not working as Mr Green's assistant.
5. they don't always deliver the goods promptly.

3.8 Three messages

The missing information is in **bold writing:**

1

SUSAN GRANT of Richmond Studios called about order for 1 x MQ 20, sent 3 weeks ago – on **5th** of this month
Sent you cheque for £425 + VAT (i.e. £**488.75**) to get it at special offer price but no **acknowledgment** of order.
Please confirm receipt of order and special **price**.
Any problems, phone Susan Grant on 0303 **518136**.
When can she expect **delivery**?
Address: **14** High Street, Woodbridge, **Ipswich**, IP12 4SJ.

2

PETER **REDFORD** of Eastern Enterprises in **Boston** called.
Can't **make it to meeting** on **Friday** afternoon because of problem with hotel – no room because of **fire**.
All other hotels in town full because of **convention**.
Will come on Monday morning (**23rd**) if OK with you.
Please tell him if this change of date is **not OK**.
Please call him if you have ideas for **solving accommodation problem** on 617 **032 0876**.

3

ALEX BROWN called:
Staying 2 extra days in **Los Angeles** and trying to get flight back on **14th**. Direct flight is full – they've put him on **the waiting list**.
May not be back till **Wednesday 17th**.
If not back, please take over at meeting on Tuesday with **Orion International**.
All info in file on his desk with **Olivia Flaubert**'s name on.
Please collect O.F. from **Talbot** Hotel first thing in the morning.
Any problem: leave a message at his hotel (**213 666 4529**) or send fax (**213 875 4114**).

4 Reports and summaries

4.1 A company report

A

(The syllable which is underlined is stressed by the speaker.)

1 business
2 products
3 market
4 leader
5 entered
6 seventies
7 develop
8 copying
9 concept
10 reliability
11 friendliness
12 office
13 specialized
14 direct
15 service

Report 1

Océ
has been in the reprographic business
for nearly seventy years,
manufacturing innovative products
for the design engineering
and office copying market.
Today

Océ is the world leader
in this market.
In the mid-sixties,
Océ first entered the fast-growing copying market.
And in the early seventies,
Océ was the first European company
to design,
develop,
manufacture
and market
its own plain-paper copying technology.
Our unique concept
was a response to buyer needs,
bringing greater reliability,
higher-quality output,
exceptional user-friendliness
and operational ease.
Océ also entered certain segments
of the office automation market,
with highly specialized marketing
and our own direct sales
and service organizations.

C

Report 3

The Swedish-based Electrolux Group
is one of the world's leading manufacturers
of household appliances.
The Group also holds a strong position in
world markets
for commercial appliances,
chainsaws
and car safety belts.
Sales in nineteen eighty-six rose by thirty-four per cent
to fifty-three thousand and ninety million
Swedish kronor
primarily as a result of the acquisition of
White Consolidated, USA,
and the consolidation of Zanussi,
an Italian white-goods company.
Despite extensive restructuring costs
and an unfavourable trend for the U.S.
dollar,
income after financial items was
maintained at the level of the previous
year.

Report 4

Brown Boveri
is a Swiss-based
mechanical,
electrical
and electronic
engineering company.
Operating worldwide
with one hundred thousand employees,
it has factories,
sales companies,
technical offices
and agencies
in some one hundred and forty countries.
Its main fields of activity
are products,
systems
and installations
for the generation,
distribution
and utilisation of electrical energy
and the related
automation,
protection
and control facilities.
In nineteen eighty-six
sales increased to thirteen point eight billion
Swiss Francs,
and orders received
to eleven billion Swiss Francs.
Net earnings were ninety-six million
Swiss Francs.
Almost eight per cent of the sales total
is spent on R & D.
Research topics include electronics,
information technologies
and process engineering.

4.2 A report

[Model report]

To: Ms Renoir, Managing Director
From: (your name)

<u>Office health and safety provisions</u>

1 As requested by the managing director on 30 March 19xx, I have investigated the problems which have been raised concerning office health and safety. In particular, I was asked to talk to the office managers and the union representatives about any accidents or job-related illnesses which may have happened and to make a number of proposals/recommendations on how best to improve the situation.

2 A study was made of all reported accidents during the past year. The accidents reported on during the year had three main causes.
   1 Faulty equipment. In two cases the lack of servicing facilities may have been responsible for the faults.
   2 A number of cases were reported of safety regulations not being followed.
   3 New staff did not know about health and safety procedures in their departments.

3 A study was also made of all job-related illnesses reported during the past year.

4 Meetings were held with union representatives and office managers to discuss what could be done.

<u>Proposals</u>

1 The safety regulations should be clearly displayed in the company's canteen and main offices.

2 Newly appointed staff should be made aware of the company's safety regulations and policy.

3 It should be the responsibility of the Personnel Manager to instruct all new staff on the procedures to be followed concerning handling of office equipment and securing of electronic and mechanical machinery.

4 First-aid drill should be practised at least once every 6 months.

5 The union suggested that substandard furniture and equipment should be replaced. In particular
   a)old -fashioned screens should be replaced – they cause eyesight problems.
   b)office lighting should be carefully checked – staff have complained of headaches after work – lighting is a large part of the problem.
   c)chairs with full back supports are essential. Many staff have complained of backache.

4.3 Using the passive

A

2. Has the draft of that memorandum really been checked?
3. The notes were finally found under the filing cabinet.
4. The components will be produced at our Marseilles factory.
5. Costs would be reduced, if less paper were used.
6. All information should be noted down in important conversations.
7. The memo to the staff committee was improved in a number of ways to make it easier to understand.
8. The mailing address was not included in the letter.
9. Suggestions should be made in writing to the personnel manager.
10. The call wasn't put through, although we had asked them to make sure it was.

B

2. The suppliers will make further modifications to this service for other customers.
3. Ordinary office staff can easily operate the machines.
4. You can place the new generation of PCs comfortably on your desk.
5. The microchip has increased the power, reliability and flexibility of computers.
6. The department now sends out standard letters a week earlier.
7. You can only achieve better results if you work harder.
8. We shall introduce the new note-taking method in our office.
9. I should warn you about the dangers of not cooperating with the personnel manager.
10. The organizers will supply all relevant information about the meeting in advance.

4.4 Punctuation

```
To:    Managing Director
From:  Staff Training Manager
Date:  18 October

Subject: PC Users' Introductory
         Course

As requested, I enclose a copy
of the provisional programme for
the Introductory Course for PC
users. It will be held from 16
December to 20 December.

Following your secretary's
telephone call, I have set aside
a session for you to speak to
the participants. I have
scheduled this for Tuesday 17
December, starting at 3.00 pm.

I am now completing the final
planning arrangements for the
course. Accordingly, I would be
grateful if you could confirm
that the proposed time on Tuesday
will be convenient for you.

In addition, I would also
appreciate receiving any
comments you may have on the
programme by Friday of this
week, if possible.
```

4.5 Summaries and note taking

B

Summary of Conversation 3:
Samantha's colleagues seem to think she's planning to leave her job.

Summary of Conversation 4:
The two colleagues are discussing whether they can make the delivery to Tarrasco or not, or whether IBO will have to wait. They decide to deliver to Tarrasco first. The spare drivers will be able to make the delivery.

4.6 Summarizing telephone messages

A

Notes 2 go with call A3. Notes 3 with A1. Notes 5 with A2. Notes 1 and 4 are left over.

B

1

TELEPHONE NOTES

DATE .... TIME ....

MESSAGE FOR ....

FROM Hotel La Cité Montréal

MESSAGE reservation for 15-19 May no single accept twin room 35% reduction? Please confirm Tel 514-288-6666

TAKEN BY ....

2

TELEPHONE NOTES

DATE .... TIME ....

MESSAGE FOR Ms. Hungerford

FROM Hilda Memering Waldheim Chemicals Hanover

MESSAGE re telex sent yesterday We need exact name customer plus particulars past orders. Ring back data p.m. between 2.30 and 3.30

TAKEN BY ....

3

TELEPHONE NOTES

DATE .... TIME ....

MESSAGE FOR Kari Hallström

FROM Roger Smiley, TMB Engineering Birmingham

MESSAGE re January shipment pls increase to 15 packets item N346 not 10 as ordered. In case of queries ring back today before 5 p.m. Tel 021-643-6891

TAKEN BY ....

4.7 Vocabulary

15 circular letter

1 recipient
2 submit
3 brief
4 executive
5 summarize
6 classify
7 draft
8 paragraph

9 colon
10 check
11 apostrophe
12 accurate
13 memorandum
14 period

5 The place of work

5.1 Prepositions – 1

2. based on
3. approved of
4. advertise for
5. account for
6. applies to
7. apply to
8. benefit from
9. applied for
10. blamed . . . for
11. arise from
12. apologized for
13. backlog of
14. bid . . . for

5.2 Agreeing and disagreeing

Conversation 1
TOPIC: It's time that smoking was forbidden once and for all in all offices.

	agrees	disagrees
1st woman	√	
1st man	√	
2nd woman		×
2nd man		×
3rd man	√	
3rd woman	√	

Conversation 2
TOPIC: All companies should offer their employees free lunches.

	agrees	disagrees
1st man	√	
1st woman	√	
2nd man		×
2nd woman	√	
3rd man	√	
4th man	√	
3rd woman		×

Conversation 3
TOPIC: Overtime should be abolished so that people without jobs can find work.

	agrees	disagrees
1st man	√	
1st woman	√	
2nd man		×
2nd woman		×
3rd man		×
4th man	√	
3rd woman	√	

Conversation 4
TOPIC: Managers should have far more control over what employees do.

	agrees	disagrees
1st man	√	
1st woman	√	
2nd man		×
2nd woman		×
3rd woman	√	
3rd man		×

5.3 Prefixes – Word-building

A

mis- 7 out- 5 over- 6 multi- 4 pre- 2
sub- 3 re- 1

B

2. outgrown
3. outlived replacing
4. miscalculated
5. overcharged
6. redesign
7. multinational
8. subdivide
9. prepackaged
10. prefabricated
11. multinational subcontract

5.4 Vocabulary

14

1 involved
2 limited
3 catering
4 retailing

5 enterprise
6 merge
7 premises
8 prosperous
9 terminals
10 modem
11 bookkeeping
12 monitor
13 corporation

5.5 Referring to the past

A

1. *JOANNA* was born in Binghampton, USA.
2. From 1980–1983 she did/studied business (studies) at the University of Potsdam.
3. Then from 1983–1985 she worked for Brown Electronics.
4. She has been working at Biofoods since 1986.
5. She has been working as export manager since 1988.
6. And she is now responsible for Scandinavia.
7. *RENATE* was born in Karlsruhe in 1959.
8. She studied Economics and Computing at the University of Munich from 1979 to 1985.
9. In 1987 she joined Biofoods as a computer operator.
10. Since 1988 she has been a trainee manager.
11. She has been responsible for Southern Europe, since February.
12. *PIERRE* was born in Amiens in 1945.
13. He served in the French Army from 1964 to 1966.
14. From 1966 to 1972 he studied electrical engineering at the University of Nantes.
15. After this he worked for General Electronics in San Diego, USA from 1973 to 1975.
16. He became an export salesman for Atlantic Refrigeration in Brest in 1975.
17. In 1977 he left and joined Biofoods France.
18. In 1980 he transferred to Basel.
19. He has been head of Export sales since 1984.

B

1. introduced
2. were took/received
3. did ... visit/go to 've ... been
4. 've ... completed/opened/set up
5. worked opened/started
6. Have ... made haven't been
7. arrived/landed kept
8. was holding/was having
9. sent hasn't made (US: didn't make)
10. was working increased/fell

5.6 Asking for information on a company

[Model Letter]

Date

Luxor International AB,
Marketing Communications
Lighting Division,
PO Box 673,
Jönköping,
Sweden

Dear Sir or Madam,

Our company is currently considering the possibility of seeking a partner in the area of electrical lighting.

Your advertisement in Newsweek recently attracted our attention. We would be very glad to have information about your company's activities.

In particular, we would

```
appreciate receiving a copy of
your advertised brochure.
   We thank you in advance for
your trouble.
   Yours faithfully,

   Your Name

   (Light Imports)
```

5.7 Telework

A

1. United States, Britain, Germany, Sweden.
2. The former networker seems to be positive. The experience of the German word processor operator seems to have been negative.

B

1. about 10,000 people at home between 2 and 4 days a week
2. how much planning the company has put into the whole program
3. reduced office-based costs improved productivity
4. greater sense of independence
5. people will have to work too much for themselves
6. within the family, within the domestic scene
7. social interaction self-disciplined professional development
8. they had no other option option would have been unemployment
9. ideal place to work the most stimulating of places to be from the point of view of personal contact

6 Import and export

6.1 Making enquiries on the phone

B

Note that this model version of the telex contains no abbreviations. Some companies may prefer to use fewer words in such a message.

```
TO MR CHAN, ORION ELECTRONICS

RE OUR ORDER NUMBER 355

GOOD MORNING. WE HAVE A
NUMBER OF QUESTIONS ABOUT THIS
ORDER:

1. HOW MANY SEPARATE
CONSIGNMENTS WILL THERE BE?
2. WHAT DATE WILL THE FIRST
CONSIGNMENT BE SHIPPED?
3. WHAT IS THE EXPECTED DATE
OF ITS ARRIVAL HERE?
4. WHAT IS THE NAME AND
PHONE NUMBER OF YOUR FREIGHT
FORWARDERS?
5. WHAT ARE THE DIMENSIONS AND
WEIGHT OF EACH PACKAGE?

PLEASE NOTE THAT OUR MR FIELD
IS IN HONG KONG NEXT WEEK. HE
WILL CALL YOU TO ARRANGE A
MEETING.

LOOKING FORWARD TO HEARING
FROM YOU.
BEST WISHES,
```

6.2 What do they want to know?

A

The correct answers are:

2 a   3 a   4 a
5 a and b   ←note *both* correct here
6 b   7 b   8 c

B

The correct answers are:
1 c 2 c 3 a 4 c 5 b – the error is in '*the latter*', i.e. the last one mentioned

6.3 Vocabulary – 1

16

1	quotation
2	invoice
3	purchase
4	documents
5	destination
6	proforma
7	forward
8	dimensions
9	freight
10	supplies
11	shipping
12	deliver
13	retail
14	overseas
15	down payment

6.4 'J.I.T.'

B

The points that were mentioned were:
1 3 5 7 9 10 12 13 15

C

Complete transcript with missing words in **bold print**

'Most major companies obtain materials from over **2000** different suppliers. With J.I.T. this number has to be cut down to around **200**. The **benefit** to the supplier is that he will get more **orders** from you if he can work with you in this way. Inevitably, this involves very close **cooperation** on the **design** and **quality** of the materials he supplies and he must adopt the J.I.T. philosophy in his own **plant**. If not, he'll find that the **pressure** is on him to hold **stock** for his customers – and this will clearly not be **economic**. If a supplier can't **cope** with J.I.T., then he'll find that **major** companies will simply find other suppliers who can.'

6.5 Prepositions – 2

2. compensate you for
3. cope with
4. convenient for
5. consent to
6. comment on
7. credit your account with
8. comply with
9. conclude from
10. cater for
11. combines elegance with
12. coordinate our activities with
13. cooperate with
14. collaborating with
15. cut back on
16. capable of
17. consists of
18. convince them of

6.6 Air freight or road transport?

A	1	B	5	C	4	D	3
E	8	F	2	G	7	H	6

6.7 The future

These are suggested answers and some variations are possible.

A

2. Tomorrow, I'**m going to ask** the boss for a rise and that's definite!
3. By the time I retire, **I'll have been working** here for 10,000 working days.
4. She'**s flying** to Spain on Tuesday to meet our clients in Seville.
5. **I'll put** the documents in the post to you first thing tomorrow.

6. Please don't disturb me for the next half hour, **I'm going to phone** Tokyo.
7. Excuse me Mr Grey, when **will** you **write** to our Norwegian clients?
8. While you **are** in Stockholm, **will** you **be seeing** Mr Olsson?
9. Stand back, everyone, he looks as if he's **going to sneeze**!
10. Don't worry, I'm sure the spare parts **will arrive** soon.

B

2. When does the plane from Bombay land here?
3. What is she going to apply for?
4. How long will you be staying there?
5. When are you going to stop work this afternoon?

C

2. Oh no, they aren't going to be rejected, they're going to be accepted.
3. Oh no, he won't still be working on it, he'll have finished it.
4. Oh no, I don't start work quite late, I start work quite early.
5. Oh no, it isn't going to run reliably, it's going to break down.

6.8 Measurements

10

1 horsepower
2 gallon
3 yard
4 feet
5 inch
6 ounce
7 hundredweight
8 pounds
9 dozen

6.9 Thank you for your order...

12 April 19--

Dear Mr Stafford,

Your Order #767 999 for ten CX 99 processors

I am sorry to inform you that we have been unable to process this order and I am returning it to you for your attention.

There has been an upgrade of the CX 99, now renamed the CX 99GT, which significantly enhances its performance and reliability. Unfortunately, this upgraded product carries with it a price increase to $145.75 per item. The original version is no longer available at the old price of $109.50. Prices of equipment and specifications are constantly changing and these are not always reflected in our advertisements, which are prepared some months before they appear in the press.

We consider the new product to be well worth the extra money.

Please let us know if you wish to proceed with the order at the new price. If you would like any more information, do please call me.

I look forward to hearing from you,

Sincerely,

7 Money matters

7.1 Reported speech

The underlined forms have been transformed or added.

Anna Braun wondered whether he thought it could have been delayed.
Bill Armstrong thought it was difficult to say. In fact he had no delivery note and no other record of its arrival.
Anna Braun wondered whether it could already have been delivered, without his knowing about it.
Bill Armstrong agreed that was perhaps true. And he asked whether they had already delivered it.
Anna Braun confirmed this. She already had their copy of the delivery note. According to that it had been delivered the month before on March 15th.
Bill Armstrong said he was sure there had been some mistake. He thought it had probably got held up in their warehouse or something.
Anna Braun said that the problem was that they had no record of payment. And that was the reason why she was ringing that day.
Bill Armstrong said that he understood completely.
Anna Braun emphasized that Bill Armstrong's firm had always been such regular payers in the past.
Bill Armstrong agreed. He wondered whether they couldn't have a little extension of credit, on that occasion.
Anna Braun stressed that she had to be honest. That would be very inconvenient.
Bill Armstrong said that they had a cash flow problem at the moment. They also had a large customer who had not paid for an order. And they hadn't budgeted for it happening.
Anna Braun said she understood.
Bill Armstrong asked whether she could let them have just ten days. And then the cheque would be on the way.
Anna Braun agreed. But she wanted to make absolutely certain that they would receive it.
Bill Armstrong added that, even if they didn't get paid themselves, he was sure they would be able to get their bank to give them an overdraft.
Anna Braun certainly hoped that would be the case.

7.2 Numbers and figures

B

The missing figures are underlined.

Profit before tax at £210.4m was ahead by 10.6% on turnover of £2,126.1m, up by 4.6%.

We must allow for the 1984 review of chemists' labour and overhead costs, as well as the net impact of currency fluctuations. Adjusting for these, profits were ahead by 12.8% on turnover up by 7.3%.

Retail Division turnover at £1,832m increased by 4.2%, and profits at £130.7m were up by 11.1%. UK sales and profits increased by 5.5% and 10.6% respectively, before property disposal surpluses.

Industrial Division achieved sales of £404.9m, an increase of 5.7%, with profits of £66.6m, ahead by 3.7%. At comparative exchange rates these increases become 11% and 15.6% respectively. The UK retail sales increased by 5.5% from an unchanged sales area.

7.3 Request for extension of credit

[Model letter]

Dynamite Developments
Malmö
Sweden

21 June 19xx

Dear Mr Ericsson,

In our telephone call of 14 June we drew your attention to a number of difficulties we have had lately with several large customers. One of the most serious results of this development has been a cash-flow problem, which means that the payment of a certain number of outstanding accounts may well have to be briefly delayed.

We are terribly sorry that Dynamite Developments has unfortunately been affected by these developments.

As you can imagine we are very eager to avoid unnecessary delay. We feel able to settle our debts very soon.

We are sure that it would not be in your interest, if the liquidation of our company became necessary.

I promise to keep you informed of further developments in the course of this month.

Yours sincerely,

....

7.4 Suffixes

B

2. monthly
3. stylish
4. affordable
5. financial
6. comfortable
7. quarterly
8. discretionary
9. vocational
10. profitable
11. cautionary
12. optional
13. concessionary
14. statistical
15. systematic

7.5 Reminding customers of non-payment of bills

A

The **credit controller** is:

VERY POLITE	POLITE	NEUTRAL	IMPOLITE	VERY IMPOLITE
1		3 4		2

The **customer**:

VERY POLITE	POLITE	NEUTRAL	IMPOLITE	VERY IMPOLITE
2	1 4			3

B

friendly	1
unfriendly	2 and 3
change	4

C

These are possible answers (we can never know for sure):
the customer probably
- paid next day in 2
- got an extension of credit in 4
- paid a week later in 1
- never did business again in 3

D

1. F
2. T
3. F
4. T
5. T
6. F (it's the March delivery)
7. F (Mr Rodrigues)
8. F (credit transfer)
9. F (it's the autumn delivery)
10. T

7.6 Prepositions – 3

1. invest in
2. involved in
3. interfere with
4. inferior to
5. introduced to
6. have a look at
7. dispose of
8. give priority to
9. have a look for
10. equivalent to
11. have confidence
12. insure against
13. engaged to
14. has been dealing with

7.7 Vocabulary

13

1	debit
2	dividend
3	bankruptcy
4	overdue
5	assets
6	charge
7	invoices
8	overheads
9	debts
10	fiscal
11	turnover
12	inflation

7.8 Taking a message – numbers

1

1000111000111	Invoice No. 5968	
	Job Reference 1 77 205039	
Marks & Numbers Not Given		
QTY	DESCRIPTION	Unit Cost
26	Model 4 Phasers Type 4/7A	$14.25 cents

2

1000111000111	Invoice No. 1450468	
	Job Reference 287456398	
Marks & Numbers HAWB 135 76		
QTY	DESCRIPTION	Unit Cost
250	Artemis Type 66A plus batteries	$58.75cents

4

1000111000111	Invoice No. 986 45	
	Job Reference 365 776	
Marks & Numbers 3 packages		
QTY	DESCRIPTION	Unit Cost
475	Type D 89 switches	5 deutschmarks each

3

1000111000111	Invoice No. GR 375	
	Job Reference 91 / 754	
Marks & Numbers 1 package		
QTY	DESCRIPTION	Unit Cost
100 sheets	Type 4479 44 x 72 cm heavy paper	$22 and 35cents

8 Delivery and after-sales

8.1 What's the problem?

1 a 2 b 3 d 4 f 5 i
6 h 7 l 8 k 9 o 10 n

8.2 What would you say?

3. I'm terribly sorry I wasn't able to call you back yesterday. It was impossible to get through because all the lines were busy.
4. I'm awfully sorry, Mr Brown. I'm afraid I misunderstood your instructions and mailed the wrong documents to our supplier.
5. Excuse me, Mr Brown, but you know those sales figures you gave me? Well, I seem to have mislaid them.
6. I'm very sorry about this, but I'm afraid we put the wrong date on the invoice we sent you, so we're sending you a new one.
7. That's quite all right. I've only been waiting about a quarter of an hour.
8. You remember that instruction manual I asked you to send us? Well, it still hasn't arrived. Could you send it quickly, please?
9. Excuse me, Mr Brown, you said you'd call our clients in Dallas. Is there still time this afternoon?
10. Oh, I'm very sorry to hear that, Mr King. I'll check it myself personally and call you back before lunch.

8.3 Vocabulary

16

1	minor
2	inferior
3	compensate
4	claim
5	install
6	arisen
7	shortage
8	warranty
9	guarantee
10	emergency
11	spare parts
12	regardless
13	maintaining
14	cautious
15	merchandise

8.4 Only the best is good enough . . .

B

The missing words are underlined:

The Quality concept can be applied to both the service sector and the manufacturing sector.
Quality affects all the functions of the company and all the staff from board level down to line managers and employees.
The key idea is 'Zero Defects' – the company should be aiming to produce goods that are perfect.
Customers should be entirely satisfied with the product.

IN THE PAST: goods were not mass-produced to a very high standard. Some faulty goods reached the customer because a complete quality control check of every manufactured item would have been too expensive. Quality control consisted of random checks.

Customers expected some faults, which could be corrected later by complaining to the supplier, who would repair or replace the faulty goods.
NOW: people believe that Quality is important because:
a) Putting mistakes right is labour-intensive and costly. It's more cost-effective to produce a perfect product with zero defects.
b) If your competitors produce goods with zero defects, your customers will prefer those. This applies to services too – your service has to be so good that your clients are entirely satisfied and there are no complaints because of defects in your product or your service.

You don't have control over your supplier, but you can change suppliers to get high quality materials. This will mean paying more, but the extra cost is justified if your own production quality improves.
If you're getting poor quality materials from a single source, you may have to start looking for alternative suppliers, or only accept supplies that are of high enough quality.
To introduce Quality you must sell the idea to everyone in the company.
Everyone has to believe in Quality.
New staff can be trained relatively easily, but established staff are harder to persuade about new ideas. Staff must take a pride in their work.
If the company can't sell its service or product, it'll lose business and people will lose jobs.

8.5 I am writing to you . . .

Dear Customer,

I am writing to you to explain the reasons for the very poor service we have given over the past few months. You may have received incomplete consignments. You may have written and not yet received a reply. You may have tried to call us and not been able to get through. We have ten Customer Service lines with staff to man them, but once these lines are overloaded there is nothing we can do. Our correspondence staff are working all hours to catch up.

The real problem goes back a long way and relates to our growth from a small family firm into a sizeable business. Our working procedures have basically not kept up with our expansion.

Last year, our old computer was replaced with new hardware and software, which we were told would solve all our problems and could expand as our business expanded. Unfortunately, this was not the case and the speed of processing orders slowed down, even though our staff were working round the clock.

We were just about to abandon the system and revert to our old procedures for processing orders when a new version of the software was supplied. This speeded up the system and we are now catching up with the backlog of orders. By the end of the month we will be completely up to date.

I know you don't want to hear about our problems. You want your orders to be delivered promptly and correctly. I promise you that in future you can rely on us to do this and to respond to your enquiries courteously and efficiently.

I feel that we owe you an apology but actions speak louder than words. We have taken on more staff, we have acquired a new warehouse and have invested heavily in computer systems, all to provide the service which you need and of which we can feel proud.

To end on a positive note, our new catalogue is enclosed and I am sure you will agree that our new product range is even more attractive and better value than before. We are working hard to continue to improve our service and I hope we can count on your support in spite of our recent problems.

Yours sincerely,

8.6 What if . . . ?

Suggested answers (many variations are possible):

A

2. How would you feel if you were promoted?
3. What would you do if you were going to America to work?
4. Where would you go if you won a lot of money?
5. What would you do if you owned your own company?
6. What would you do if tomorrow was a day off?

B

2. But if they hadn't installed a new computer, things wouldn't have got worse.
3. But if the software had been tested, the system wouldn't have broken down.
4. But if orders hadn't been delayed, customers wouldn't have complained.
5. But if the phone lines hadn't been overloaded, customers would have been able to get through.
6. But if there hadn't been a lot of / so many problems, customers wouldn't have looked for a more reliable supplier.

C

2. in case
3. unless
4. when
5. if (or when)
6. until

8.7 Prepositions – 4

2. negotiating with
3. make a large profit on
4. put pressure on
5. placed an order for   with
6. lack of
7. proportion of
8. I object to
9. merged with
10. notify us of
11. We're looking forward to
12. proceeds of
13. line of
14. purchased this product from
15. order larger quantities from

8.8 Take a message

A

The missing words are in **bold writing**:

Call from **Henri Morand, Transocéan S.A., Bordeaux**.

- Both AR 707's running for 6 weeks now. Usual routine tests done before installing them in labs but now one unit is **noisy**.
- Makes a loud harsh **vibrating** noise, as if drive motor is **unbalanced** or one of the heads touching **side of case**. Happens **2 or 3 times** a day After **30 secs**. noise stopped and **readings** normal.
- Question: is this a fault they **should worry about**?
  If it _is_ a problem that needs fixing they can **send the unit back**. Please confirm that this will be **at our expense** and they can have **replacement unit immediately**.
- Or they have unit examined by local **expert – at our expense**.
- Call him **at home** tomorrow a.m. on **56 52 60 44**.

B

Model telex to Mr Morand:

```
TO HENRI MORAND
FROM (your name)

I AM SORRY TO HEAR OF YOUR PROBLEMS
WITH ONE OF YOUR AR 707 UNITS. I
DON'T THINK YOU NEED TO WORRY
ABOUT THE VIBRATING NOISE. BUT TO
SET YOUR MIND AT REST WE HAVE
INSTRUCTED OUR AGENT TO VISIT YOU
NEXT WEEK TO EXAMINE THE UNIT.
OUR AGENT, ACE IMPORTERS, WILL BE
IN TOUCH WITH YOU ON MONDAY.
BEST WISHES,
```

C

Call from Byron Santini, Sunrise Electronics, Toledo, Ohio.

- He's sent us 2 telexes and 1 fax but no reply from us.
- Re: upgrade of 4 x Sunrise 3 Drives with new hardware options.
- He understood we would ship them at our expense, then they would upgrade for $250 per unit, then ship them back to us at their expense.
- This arrangement confirmed in our fax to them of July 7.
- Problems:
  1. They've only received 1 drive.
  2. We've charged their agents here for air freight and insurance
- Proposal:
  They will upgrade drive number R 9290004 and charge us for air freight and insurance. Please confirm this is acceptable.
- Question:
  Were other 3 drives sent at the same time?
  If so, maybe lost in transit.
  If not, send them right away but at our firm's expense.

Call him tomorrow before 6 pm their time (419 897 4567) or send fax (419 897 0982).

N.B. If they don't hear from us, they'll hold the one drive they've received and withdraw special price of $250 for the upgrade!

D

Model fax to Mr Santini:

Dear Mr Santini,

Thank you for your telephone message. I apologize for the misunderstanding about shipping costs and for your lack of success in getting in touch with me: both of these are due to an epidemic of flu that has left us short-staffed and which kept me in bed for ten days.

We accept your proposal to upgrade drive number R 9290004 and charge us for air freight and insurance.

The remaining three drives have not yet been packed and shipped. As soon as we have received back the first drive and it is running again, we will send them to you at our expense.

Thank you for your patience.

Sincerely,

9 Visits and travel

9.1 Did I ever tell you about ... ?

Correct sequence of pictures:

for story A:
2 1 4 3

for story B:
2 1 5 4 3

for story C:
1 3 2

9.2 Prepositions – 5

2. reminds me of
3. retired from
4. resigned from
5. report on
6. running short of
7. remit . . . to
8. regardless of
9. qualified for
10. range from . . . to
11. reduction in
12. responsible for
13. ran out of
14. report to

9.3 Air travel in the USA

B

2. fly to Orange County (John Wayne Airport) or Hollywood-Burbank Airport.
3. wait for your plane.
4. won't be any cheaper.
5. avoid a busy gateway like New York, Miami or Los Angeles – Charlotte, Pittsburgh and Orlando are less busy.

C

1. be delayed because too many flights are scheduled to take off around that time.
2. get anything to drink or eat.
3. frightened, especially if you're in the clouds.
4. you get a guaranteed seat and a free phone call to the person who is meeting you the other end.
5. airports will be especially busy.
6. O'Hare (Chicago), Atlanta or Denver.
7. check it in – take it as hand baggage.
8. something to eat and drink in your hand luggage.

9.4 -ing v. to . . .

2. to seeing
3. to wear
4. booking
5. Driving
6. standing
7. to stay
8. to discover
9. to make
10. to receive
11. to admire
12. Travelling
13. to let me know
14. smoking
15. to go
16. to get
17. to import
18. jogging
19. to swim
20. to call
21. meeting
22. waiting
23. finding
24. to survive

9.5 What would you say?

Suggested answers:

2. I'd like to change my reservation on flight LJ 879 on May 16 to flight ZZ 857 on the next day.
3. Is it too early to check in for flight RA 372?
4. Excuse me, could you show me how to get a ticket from this machine?
5. The main railway station? Yes, you go down this road for two blocks and then turn left. You can't miss it.
6. I'm terribly sorry I'm so late. I rented a car and it wouldn't start, you see.
7. Could you explain some of these dishes on the menu for me, please?
8. I'd like to have just a plain omelette, if that's all right.
9. Can you recommend a nice local dish?
10. Oh, do let me pay for this, please.

9.6 Vocabulary

16

1 visa
2 economy
3 hire
4 transfer
5 postponed
6 route
7 bill
8 fuel
9 rented

10 conference
11 translator
12 interpreter
13 delegates
14 check in
15 convention

C

Complete text:

Presenter:
I think the worst parts of a trip are having to travel overnight or get up at 3 am to catch an early flight, or being stuck for a weekend in some dreadful industrial city. Are there any ways of avoiding that?

Nigel:
Mm, yes, a weekend break or a stopover in a more relaxing or lively city is often available at a special cheap weekend rate. Various airlines and hotel chains offer these and it's always more pleasant to stay the night in a hotel than on a plane, even if you're in business class. For example, for no extra charge you can spend an evening somewhere nice like Copenhagen, Madrid or Vienna before a long-haul flight the next morning.

9.7 What the clever traveller knows

B

2. keeping them in your hand luggage.
3. buying an RTW (round the world) ticket.
4. buying a ticket to Buenos Aires and not using the Rio-Buenos Aires leg.
5. a flight to Japan via Bahrain, Hong Kong and Taipeh.
6. staying away for more than two weeks.
7. allow time for delays and breakdowns.
8. get to know a good travel agent.
9. avoid.
10. finding out which airlines offer a free seat for your spouse.
11. getting rooms at a discount through your travel agent.
12. staying there regularly and becoming eligible for 'special customer status'.

9.8 Negative prefixes

B

un-
unemployed
unforeseen
unused
unreadable
undesirable
unknown
unfortunately

dis-
dishonest
dissatisfied
disconnect

in-
informal
inexperienced
inconvenient
invalid
incapable
insufficient

non-
non-stop
non-payment
non-union
non-profit-making

C

anti-union
semi-circle
anti-government
semi-professional
semi-official
semi-permanent
semi-automatic

D

The missing words are:

2. non-stop
3. insufficient
4. illegal
5. dissatisfied
6. invisible
7. anti-clockwise/counter-clockwise
8. invalid
9. Unfortunately
10. unforeseen

---

10 Marketing and sales

10.1 Comparison

A

2.	worse	the worst
3.	more badly (or worse)	the most badly (or the worst)
4.	more basic	the most basic
5.	busier (or more busy)	the busiest (or the most busy)
6.	darker	the darkest
7.	easier	the easiest
8.	more efficient	the most efficient
9.	faster	the fastest
10.	better	the best
11.	happier	the happiest
12.	noisier (or more noisy)	the noisiest (or the most noisy)
13.	more pleased	the most pleased
14.	more reliable	the most reliable
15.	more serious	the most serious
16.	stiffer	the stiffest
17.	more useful	the most useful
18.	more useless	the most useless
19.	better	the best
20.	more willing	the most willing

B

2. All the other products are more expensive than ours.
3. There aren't as many competing brands on the market as there were ten years ago.
4. Three times as many consumers prefer our product to theirs.
5. The least important feature of the product is its colour.
6. The price is just as important as the design to our customers.
7. Their product costs a little more than ours does.
8. Our product is far more attractive than theirs.
9. It isn't quite as easy to service the new model as the old one.
10. Our product is more reliable than theirs.
11. Most of the competing brands are less widely available than our product.
12. Quality is more important than price, as far as our customers are concerned.

10.2 Vocabulary – 1

20

1 forecast
2 label
3 launch
4 chart
5 consumer
6 graph
7 poster
8 display

9 trademark
10 bargain
11 media

12 brands
13 survey
14 design
15 region
16 fluctuate
17 sales drive
18 statistics
19 chain store

10.3 Prepositions – 6

2. wasting ... on
3. transmit ... to
4. take into consideration
5. submit ... to
6. withdraw from
7. superior to
8. speed up
9. scheduled for
10. share ... with
11. specializes in
12. valid for
13. write off
14. take over from

10.4 Vocabulary – 2

9 (down): monopoly

1 sample
2 boost
3 trend
4 worldwide
5 competitor
6 volume
7 goodwill
8 publicity

10.5 The three stages of a sales interview

A

1. product
2. weaknesses
3. buying
4. before
5. wants and needs
6. client
7. individual

B

The missing words are in CAPITAL LETTERS:

1. The OPENING Stage: usually a phone call.
   You have to talk to YOUR CLIENT in person – not his/her SECRETARY
   Identify yourself and arrange an APPOINTMENT
2. The BUILDING Stage:
   a) prepare and REHEARSE with a FRIEND or RELATION
   b) dress SUITABLY FOR THE OCCASION
   c) behave in a FRIENDLY, CONFIDENT BUT BUSINESSLIKE manner
   d) don't spend too long on SOCIAL CONVERSATION
   e) show that you're a RESPONSIBLE, TRUSTWORTHY person
   f) mention WELL-KNOWN firms who use your product
   g) tell the client about the BENEFITS of your product
   h) encourage your client to ASK QUESTIONS and only talk HALF the time yourself
3. The CLOSING Stage: recognizing exactly when your client is ready to PLACE the order. This depends on TIMING.
   Finally, THANK your client for the order and leave.

C

1. × not covered
2. × not covered
3. × not covered
4. √ covered
5. × not covered
6. √ covered
7. √ covered
8. × not covered

10.6 How certain are they?

B

100% (certain) Betty
75% (likely)
50% (possible) Diana
25% (unlikely) Alan
0% (impossible) Christian
Eric doesn't know

C

100% (certain)	Alan
75% (likely)	Eric
50% (possible)	Betty
25% (unlikely)	Christian
0% (impossible)	Diana

D

100% (certain)	Alan
75% (likely)	Eric
50% (possible)	Diana, Christian
25% (unlikely)	
0% (impossible)	Betty

11 Meetings

11.1 What would you say?

Suggested answers:

2. Do you see what I mean?
3. Could I make a suggestion? Would this be a good time to adjourn for lunch?
4. All right, ladies and gentlemen, shall we take a vote on this?
5. All right, ladies and gentlemen, are we unanimous on this? Good, then let's move on to the next item.
6. I'm sorry, that's not really my field. I don't have any strong feelings on it.
7. Miss Frost, what do you think about this?
8. I agree entirely with Mrs Collins, it seems to me that...
9. I don't quite agree with Mr Davies's point. In fact, I'd say that...
10. I'm sorry, would you excuse me for a moment? I need to go to the toilet.

11.2 About this meeting...

To Mr Hanson

Ingrid Muster called from Berlin. Problem with flights : won't arrive till Friday 2.30. Apologies but unavoidable. But meeting can continue in evening. Please inform your people.

She's bringing Peter - he's done all the research, so best person to put everyone in picture. Please book 2 rooms at the Royal Hotel for night of 13th and cancel booking for night of 12th.

To Linda Taylor

Tim Hanson called re-meeting on Friday 13th. Time changed because Ingrid can't get flight from Berlin. New time: 2.30 instead of 10.30. But lunch is still on and you're welcome to join them. Please call Mrs Burrows on 345 0982 to confirm whether joining them for lunch or not.

Meeting will go on at least till 6, probably longer, so you may need to book hotel room. You can do this or call Mrs Burrows to do this for you. (Ingrid and Peter staying at Royal, near station. If full, Imperial nearby is good.)

Any problems call Mrs Burrows. Or call Mr Hanson at home this evening on 778 8021.

11.3 Vocabulary

17 (down): any other business

1. agenda
2. minutes
3. majority
4. motion
5. attend
6. chairperson
7. preliminary
8. adjourn
9. behalf
10. outcome
11. proposal
12. minority
13. unanimous
14. proposed
15. miscellaneous
16. concludes

11.4 Prepositional phrases – 1

2. at last
3. during working hours
4. by accident
5. at a loss
6. at least
7. for the benefit of
8. at cost price
9. at a bargain price
10. for cash
11. by telex
12. by letter
13. at our expense
14. at a . . . good price
15. at a profit
16. by air
17. at your disposal
18. by return of post/mail

11.5 Place and direction

A

Suggested answers:

3. Number three is behind the letter D.
4. Number four is on the left of the letter F.
5. Number five is on top of the letter E.
6. Number six is above the letter G.
7. Number seven is below the letter H.
8. Number eight is in front of the letter I.
9. Number nine is near the right-hand edge of the box, near the letter J.
10. Number ten is at the bottom of the box, near the letter K.
11. Number eleven is at the top of the box, all by itself.
12. Number twelve is beside/next to the letter L.
13. Number thirteen is to the right of the letter L near the edge of the box.
14. Number fourteen is on its own in the bottom left-hand corner of the box.
15. Number fifteen is between the letters A and B, below number one.

11.6 Choose the best summary

The best summaries are:

2 b   3 a   4 b   5 c

11.7 More suffixes

A

debtor
distributor
examiner
inspector
insurer
inventor
investigator
manufacturer
negotiator
operator
purchaser

retailer
shipper
supervisor
supplier
wholesaler

payee
licensee
consignee
employee

B

to categorize	tighten
to computerize	loosen
to privatize	harden
to nationalize	brighten
to legalize	flatten
to generalize	sharpen
to subsidize	sweeten
to specialize	
to rationalize	
to modernize	

11.8 We need some guidelines...

C

Model report:

```
A meeting was held to
determine guidelines for
anyone travelling on the
firm's behalf.

It was agreed that:
1. An advance will be paid at
   least ten days before date
   of travel. This will be the
   estimated expenses in trav-
   eller's cheques and/or cash
   plus £200 in traveller's
   cheques for emergencies.
2. The firm will be
   responsible for booking and
   paying for air tickets.
3. Short-haul flights will be
   economy class. Long-haul
   flights will be club/
   business class.
4. Travellers will be
   responsible for checking
   that the times and dates of
   flights are correct when
   they receive their tickets,
   to avoid difficulties en
   route.
5. All people involved should
   have a copy of itinerary.
6. All people involved should
   have a list of the full
   names (not just initials)
   of everyone involved and
   their addresses and phone
   numbers.
7. Accommodation will be
   booked that is central,
   comfortable and secure.
   This will not normally be
   the most expensive hotel in
   the town.
```

D

Completed transcript:

Kate: We haven't talked about the other problem that J.L. had: apparently his flight back had the wrong date on it, the 24th. He didn't notice this till the 25th, the day he was due to fly. Luckily, the flight wasn't full and they accepted the ticket with no extra charge.

David: Well, I mean, he should have checked the ticket, so that's really his own fault.

Kate: But this needs to be made clear. I don't know, maybe a covering note when we send the tickets saying 'Please check that the times and dates on these tickets are correct.'

David: Very simple. Very, very good idea. We'll do that. And someone in your department must double-check this. Do we need to make it clear that flights would normally be economy class by the cheapest route? F.E. seems to have the ... er ... F.E. seems to have the idea that he should have flown Club class.

Kate: Well, actually, normally we *would* book Club class on a long-haul flight. I think we should make this clear in the guidelines.

David: Oh well, I didn't ... I didn't even know that!

Kate: Right, anything else?

David: Er ... no, I don't think so, but let's meet again when we've circulated a report on this meeting and we've got some feedback.

Kate: OK. Can you just switch off the tape recorder?

David: Sure, I press this one, do I? Like this?

Kate: Yes. That's right.

12 Operations and processes

12.1 Prepositional phrases – 2

2. in the process of
3. in cash
4. in progress
5. in difficulties
6. in anticipation
7. in spite of
8. in accordance with
9. in bulk
10. in advance
11. in transit
12. in running/working order
13. in consultation with
14. in time for
15. in confidence
16. in charge of
17. in triplicate
18. In addition to
19. in debt
20. in a hurry

12.2 Explaining

A

Suggested answers:
2. 'Look all you do is press this button.'
3. 'That's clear, is it?'
4. 'Make sure you remember to . . .'
5. 'I wonder if I might trouble you for a moment? But . . .'
6. 'Sorry to bother you, but . . .'
7. 'How do you do that again?'
8. 'I'm sorry, could you repeat that bit again.'

B

1. using a microcomputer
2. making a paper aeroplane
3. starting a record player
4. instructions to a typist on how to type up a report

C

Perhaps some of these words helped you to understand what the person was explaining:
1. put the plug in switch switch this on
   push it into this slot to load I click
   to save use another one leaving it on
2. a piece of paper – A4 size fold it
   Next fold the point a pair of scissors
   from the nose fold down the wings
   to throw it
3. the machine is plugged in switched on
   open it up the control arm
   you want to hear the correct speed
   automatic
4. Use A4 paper one top copy
   and then two extra copies
   type in double spacing on one side of the paper only
   Don't type part of a word on one line
   Now number the pages
   a separate page for each of the tables
   Don't indent the first paragraph after a heading
   the Contents page is to be typed last

12.3 Modal verbs

A

Suggested answers:
2. The firm could build the car at this plant.
3. That could/may be why the company closed down.
4. We might/may enlarge the present site.
5. He said we could change the plan.
6. You could try to follow the instructions more closely.
7. They may use this canteen.
8. You must follow the instructions closely.
9. You have to plug the monitor in before you switch the computer on.
10. You ought to/should listen to what your boss tells you.
11. They ought to/should pay more for overtime.
12. The assembly line needn't stop/doesn't have to stop for them to do the maintenance work.

B

2. not able	8. perhaps able
3. important	9. possible
4. possible	10. essential
5. not obliged	11. perhaps
6. not right	12. right
7. necessary	

12.4 A memorandum

MEMORANDUM

From: Chief Executive
To: Production Director

<u>Proposals for machinery for Machine Shop X</u>

As you know the company is contemplating opening a new machine shop in the near future. Our operations have been expanding so rapidly that such a development now appears inevitable.

There are a number of questions which we need to be thinking about and which I would be grateful to hear your opinion on concerning the idea.

1. The choice of new machinery. I would like to know whether you think we should buy or hire new equipment.

2. Then I would like to hear your proposals on which machinery we should consider acquiring.

3. Closely connected with the purchase or hire of machinery is the matter of maintenance. We clearly need to consider the question in making our decision. Labour costs for maintenance staff will also need to be discussed. How many new staff will be required, for example?

4. At the same time I would appreciate it, if you could provide me with estimates of the probable working life of the equipment which you propose.

Could you please let me have your preliminary thoughts on the questions in time for our meeting next week?

12.5 How to fight noise

A

3

B

1 c	2 b	3 b	4 a	5 a
6 c	7 b	8 b	9 b	10 c

12.6 Vocabulary

13

1 facilitate
2 insert
3 position
4 resources
5 streamline
6 setback
7 dismantle
8 by-product

9 alter
10 maintenance
11 enlarge
12 manpower

13 A new job

13.2 Abstract nouns

Notice the spelling of the words printed in **bold letters.**

A

VERBS → NOUNS
acknowledgement, achievement, adjournment, agreement, announcement, amendment, arrangement, assessment, consignment, development, embarrassment, endorsement, enjoyment, equipment, establishment, judgement, measurement, **repayment**

adaptation, alteration, **application**, authorization, centralization, cancellation, confirmation, consultation, declaration, determination, devaluation, imagination, modification, **pronunciation**, recommendation, specialization

administration, appreciation, arbitration, automation, circulation, collaboration, cooperation, complication, concentration, calculation, elimination, fluctuation, hesitation, integration, location, speculation

attraction, collection, contribution, correction, deduction, deletion, interruption, **pollution**, prediction, protection, reduction

B

ADJECTIVES → NOUNS
calmness, carelessness, cheapness, **friendliness**, helpfulness, lateness, loudness, nervousness, seriousness

confidence, intelligence, patience, difference

capability, **flexibility**, formality, inferiority, legality, objectivity, possibility, probability, popularity, reality, **reliability**, scarcity, sincerity, superiority

13.3 An interesting job

Model letter:

```
                              3333 Imperial Way
                            · K-10004 Freetown
                                       Fredonia

Mr Charles Fox
European Sales Office
ACME Atlantic Ltd
45 Pentonville Road
London EC2 4AC

                                   13 May 19--

Dear Mr Fox,

I wish to apply for one of the
positions described in your
advertisment 'Work in Bermuda' in
this week's Daily Planet.
  My name is Jean Muster. I am 25
years old and a Fredonian
citizen. I am at present working
for Fredonian Enterprises, and as
you know, we have being doing
business with ACME Atlantic for a
number of years.
  I would be interested in a
6-month contract. During this
time my present employers are
willing to give me leave of
absence.
  My recent work has involved
working in a team in the export
department of my firm and I have
developed confidence and skill in
dealing with foreign buyers on
the telephone and in writing,
mainly using English.
  My Fredonian is fluent, I speak
and write reasonably good English
and I can also handle business
correspondence in German and
Italian.
  As you will see from my
enclosed CV, my qualifications
are good, and I think you will
agree that my experience and
language skills will help me to
```

make a valuable contribution to your firm and you will find that I am an enthusiastic and resourceful employee.

I am available for interview at any time except for June 12th to 21st. My daytime phone number is 287 8889 extension 333.

Looking forward to hearing from you,

Yours sincerely,

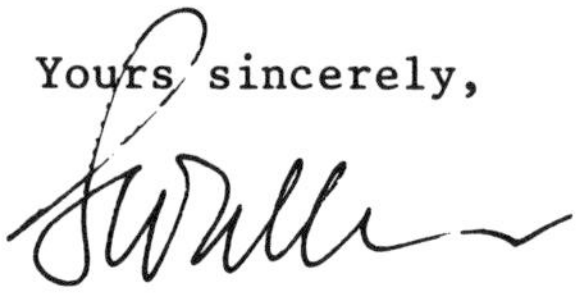

13.4 Relative clauses

A

2. Mr Wright, whose application form we received yesterday, is a very promising candidate.
3. His CV, which you showed me yesterday, is most impressive.
4. He has excellent references from his present employers who are ACME Engineering. NO COMMAS
5. He was working in Norwich, where they have their HQ.
6. His qualifications, which you commented on, are excellent.
7. The personnel officer who interviewed him says that he's available at once. NO COMMAS
8. The thing that impressed her most is his personality. NO COMMAS

B

Notice that there are commas only in 4 and 7:

2. I heard about the vacancy from a friend who works in Personnel.
3. He gave me some information that/ which was supposed to be confidential.
4. I heard about this from a colleague, who assured me it was true.
5. Apparently, we sent the forms to an address which/that was wrong.
6. The person whose name you gave as a reference is unwilling to comment on you.
7. I had to fill in a six-page application form, which was very time-consuming.
8. I applied for a job that/which I saw advertised in the newspaper.

13.5 Vocabulary

15

1	fill out
2	career
3	appoint
4	applicant
5	sought
6	wages
7	board
8	income
9	candidate
10	panel
11	self-employed
12	responsibilities
13	tax
14	salary

26

16	status
17	pension
18	permanent
19	prospects
20	challenge
21	personnel
22	temporary
23	fill in
24	vocational
25	resume

13.6 Who should we short-list?

REPORT FROM GUS MORRISON IN GLASGOW

Best candidate: Duncan McCabe, 21, graduate of Edinburgh University (MA in modern languages). Working for

publicity department of Glasgow City Council for about a year.
Speaks fluent French and quite good German.
Very pleasant, a bit shy when you first talk to him, but when you get to know him he has a lovely sense of humour.
Very bright and eager and he'd fit in well with your people down in London. Not available until September 1st.
Address: 145 Pentland Gardens,
Glasgow, GL5 876
Phone: 041 667 8092.

REPORT FROM LAURA STEELE IN SHEFFIELD

Best candidate: Mrs Sylvia Sabbatini, 25, married. Working for Johnson Bros in Marketing since leaving school.
Lovely personality – very cheerful and bright. Speaks Italian fluently (father Italian, mother English).
Paper qualifications not all that good: left school at 16 to do secretarial course, but very intelligent young woman – she impressed me very much.
Married for 2 years, no children. Husband just got a job in London, so able to start work in London right away.
Address: 70 Pennine Avenue,
Huddersfield, LS34 7QT
Phone: 0484 078432.

REPORT FROM TERRY WILLIAMS IN CARDIFF

Best candidate: Miss Emma Harris, 20, has really good potential.
Had right exam results to get into university, but decided to go into industry.
Speaks Spanish and French (not exactly fluent, but so confident this doesn't matter).
Working in marketing for small light engineering firm, became Export Marketing Manager when firm taken over and she was made redundant – they decided to close her department.
Full of confidence, makes friends easily and would work well in a team. No ties here, could start work next week if you wanted.
She'd be a real find and you should get in touch with her right away.
Address: 214 Gower Road,
Swansea, SA2 4PJ
Phone: 0792 98762.

13.7 Prepositional phrases – 3

2. on display
3. on the spot
4. on request
5. on order
6. on closer inspection
7. on the telephone
8. on approval
9. on time
10. on a ship/on a plane
11. on business
12. on vacation/on holiday
13. on condition
14. on paper
15. on loan
16. on behalf of
17. on schedule

13.8 High-flyers

B

1 a	2 c	3 a	4 b	5 c
6 c	7 b	8 b	9 c	10 c
11 b	12 b			

14 Working together

14.1 Prepositional phrases – 4

2. through the usual channels
3. of minor importance
4. under pressure
5. through official channels
6. of inferior quality
7. out of order
8. to the same effect
9. out of work
10. out of date
11. With reference to
12. of short duration
13. to a certain extent
14. out of stock

14.2 Asking for and giving advice

A

2 c	3 f	4 b	5 c	6 g	
7 b	8 e	9 b	10 e	11 c	
12 g	13 a	14 d	15 a		
16 g	17 c	18 d	19 a		
20 d	21 f	22 a			

B

Conversation 1
1. They're on first name terms. Friends.
2. The woman says she's not sure what to do now she has just got the sack.
3. The man suggests she ought to look through the adverts in the newspaper or that she could perhaps start up her own business.
4. We don't know.

Conversation 2
1. Colleagues at work.
2. One woman wonders what she should do because her boss has asked her out to dinner.
3. The second woman advises her to ring up the boss's wife and tell her about it.
4. Yes.

Conversation 3
1. Colleagues.
2. One woman wonders what she should do about the constant lateness of the girl in her office.
3. The other woman says she could talk to the girl about it.
4. Yes.

14.3 Vocabulary

17

1 benefits
2 confidential
3 dispute
4 redundancy
5 go-slow
6 incentive
7 promotion
8 maintain
9 sack
10 lay-offs

11 drawback
12 reject
13 flexitime
14 shift
15 negotiate
16 insists

14.4 Order of adverbs

A

2. European computer manufacturers are **apparently** going to work together on this project.
3. The bonus was **occasionally** much higher than the management had planned.
4. There has **definitely** been a mistake made in this invoice.
5. If the management **sincerely** want the workforce to accept their offer, they must show more flexibility.

6. We **specifically** asked to see the union representatives before we made the decision.
7. **Initially** the customer was quite satisfied with our after-sales service. (*Or:* The customer was **initially** quite satisfied with our after-sales service.)
8. The order book is **currently** stagnating. (*Or:* **Currently** the order book is stagnating.)
9. Although the freight was handled **carefully**, important components were broken in transit.
10. We have **gradually** increased our product range in order to give our customers more choice.

B

1. We are **certainly** going to investigate the whole question as soon as possible.
2. In a different economic climate the workforce would **probably** have accepted the pay deal.
3. The customers **always** complain when we send John instead of Margaret to the sales conference.
4. The managing director **often** writes in the internal newsletter about the progress the company is making.
5. The supervisor is **never** able to find somebody who is willing to stay behind to take the late overseas orders.
6. The designers have **nearly** completed the new company logo.
7. If the correct procedure is followed, you will **hardly ever** have a breakdown.
8. Our head office **almost** forgot to appoint an overseas agent for European sales.
9. The management has **just** announced the plan for rationalizing production on this site.
10. Do you think the firm will **ever** get the Chinese order?

14.5 Company training

1. Those companies whose members agree on certain fundamental values and norms are said to be more successful than those which do not.
2. Because companies need to raise productivity in an atmosphere of extremely sharp competition.
3. The employees. And customers of the company have voiced their criticisms too.
4. Breakthrough Learning and Transformational Technologies.
5. It means everyone thinks in more or less the same fashion.
6. As a kind of mind control. They say that they promote values which are against their religious beliefs.
7. All 67,000 employees.
8. Positive-thinking techniques and the importance of group cohesion.
9. duration rationality security resources position relation
10. c
11. Customers of the company say that the costs for the training are resulting in increased telephone bills.
12. A system of beliefs instead of a hierarchy built on carrots and sticks.
13. Because the programmes are so expensive and millions of dollars are being invested.

14.6 Unions and technological change

A

[Model letter]

Dear Colleague,

In 1983 our union's national banking committee published a booklet "After 1984", which outlined the systems which many large banks had already introduced or planned to introduce in the near future.

At that time, many people said our predictions were stupid and that we were exaggerating. We only wish we had been.

The banks have proceeded rapidly with the introduction of technology. But what they have not done is to demonstrate an awareness of the need to reach agreement on the effects on employment, career structure, promotion prospects or the many other aspects of working life which technology influences.

Our union is aware of the advantages and dangers of new technology. We accept that technological development will bring about changes in our industry, but we cannot accept that this change will be at the expense of our members' jobs and career prospects.

That is why we have been seeking a "New Technology Agreement" in order that changes in the banks can be introduced on a bilateral, rather than a unilateral basis.

I ask you to give your full support to our campaign and to help to explain to non-members how vital it is for them to join our union. In this way we can achieve protection for your future through agreements negotiated by a strong and independent union.

Technology can bring uncertainty and a worsening of conditions. It can also bring an improvement through a shorter working week, more employment opportunities and greater job satisfaction. The choice is yours – with us.

Yours sincerely

Frank Kelly

General Secretary

B

1 c   2 c   3 a   4 b   5 c

---

15 Revision

15.1 Grammar revision

Correct answers:

1 c   2 c   3 a   4 a   5 c
6 c   7 d   8 b   9 d   10 a
11 a   12 d   13 d   14 a
15 b   16 d   17 c   18 b
19 b   20 c

15.2 Word-building revision

1. tighten
2. flexibility
3. modernization
4. inexperienced
5. oversimplification
6. unreliable
7. repayment
8. anticlockwise
9. administrator
10. recommendation

15.3 Prepositions revision

1.	of	about	
2.	on	from/for	
3.	of	in	
4.	in	of	
5.	on	of	
6.	from	at	
7.	With	to (GB) / In	to (US)
8.	on	in	
9.	with	for	
10.	on	on	

15.4 Vocabulary revision

A	P	P	O	I	N	T	M	E	N	T	S		H	P
C		A		N		I		X		A				E
C	A	P	I	T	A	L		P	A	R	T	N	E	R
O		E		E		L		O		G				S
U		R	A	R	E		O	R	D	E	R	S		O
N				E		I		T		T		A		N
T	H	O	U	S	A	N	D				P	L	A	N
		F		T		V		E		F		E		E
S	O	F	T		P	E	N	S	I	O	N	S		L
T		I		C		S		T		O				
R	E	C	E	I	P	T		I	L	L	E	G	A	L
I		E		R		M		M				O		E
K		S	E	C	R	E	T	A	R	Y		O	W	N
E				U		N		T		E		D		D
S	I	G	N	S		T	R	E	E	S		S	T	

15.5 Functions revision

A

a 5 b 7 c 1 d 10 e 2
f 8 g 3 h 9 i 4 j 6

B

	Conversation	[1]	[2]	[3]	[4]
a)	asking permission to do something				
b)	requesting				
c)	offering to help	√			
d)	agreeing or disagreeing				
e)	asking for or giving information		√	√	
f)	complaining	√			
g)	apologizing	√			
h)	telling a story				
i)	explaining or giving instructions			√	
j)	asking for and giving advice	√			√

C

1.	a) F	b) F	c) T	d) T	e) T
2.	a) T	b) F	c) F		
3.	a) T	b) F	c) F	d) T	
4.	a) F	b) F	c) T	d) T	

D

These are only suggested answers. Many variations are possible:

1. Good morning, Mr Martin, it's nice to see you again. Did you have a good journey?
2. Yes, certainly, you can use the phone in my office. Just dial 9 for an outside line.
3. Sorry, could you say that again, please?
4. Yes I know, I'm very sorry about that. There was a slip-up in our shipping department.
5. Thanks for letting me know. I'll look into that right away.
6. I'm absolutely sure that our new product will sell well.
7. That's exactly what I think.
8. Well, the first thing you have to do is . . .
9. Well, if I were you, I'd place an order for 250, because . . .
10. Mr Martin, did I ever tell you about . . . ?

15.6 Midway International

Model letters (many variations possible):

A

Midway International

PO Box 777 K-4550 Euroville Yourland

Mrs J. McArthur
Original Products plc
20 Kirkton Campus
Livingston EH54 6QA
Scotland

April 10, 19--

Dear Mrs McArthur,

Our order MI/876

We were very dismayed to receive your letter of 2 April, announcing a delay in shipping this order. I should like to point out that we have customers waiting and that if the goods do not arrive soon, we shall have to cancel this order. It is essential that we receive the units by 1 May at the very latest.

May I ask you to make sure that you give our order top priority, as we have been loyal customers of yours for many years.

A further point in your letter gives us great concern. You say that the speed of the unit is 'slightly reduced'. In our opinion, however, the speed of the unit is considerably slower than the specification. We fear that our customers will not find this acceptable. In view of this, we suggest that your price to us should be reduced by $45 per unit.

Regarding feedback on your OP 424 series, we will ask our own customers for their comments and keep you informed. We have one OP 424 in our head office which does seem to overheat, but so far this has not broken down – yet!

We would also like to know whether, in case of breakdown, users should return the defective units directly to your factory for repair or replacement.

We look forward to hearing from you and hope you can reassure us on the points made above.

Yours sincerely,

Your name
p.p. M. Meyer

B

Midway International

PO Box 777 K-4550 Euroville Yourland

Mr Bruce Dundee,
Ultimate Pty,
4130 Pacific Drive,
Brisbane,
Australia

April 10, 19--

Dear Bruce,

Michael, who's on holiday this week, has asked me to write to warn you that your order UP/901 for 10 OP 232s is going to be delayed. We are sorry about this but there is not much we can do. The manufacturers have had some difficulties with unreliable CPUs but they have solved these problems by finding a supplier in the USA. We now plan to ship to you on 2 May by airfreight – but if we do manage to get our delivery earlier, we will put them straight on the plane to you.

I have also been asked to mention that although more reliable CPUs are being used (68000s instead of 68020s), the processing speed is reduced from 12 MHz to just under 10 Mhz. I don't think this will affect your use of the units, though. We are asking the manufacturer to reduce his prices and if he agrees to do this we will pass this saving on to you in full.

One more thing: could you give us a few comments on the OP 424 series? We would like to know your reactions to the price, packaging and design of this product. If you have had any problems with reliability, could you let us know about that too, please?

Thanks for your patience. We will send you a fax as soon as the OP 232's are ready to ship.

Best wishes to Sheila.

Yours,

Your name

Your Name
for Michael Meyer

15.7 The Peterborough Effect – 1

1 a 2 b 3 c 4 b 5 c
6 c 7 a 8 c 9 c 10 b

15.8 The Peterborough Effect – 2

1 b 2 a 3 b 4 a 5 b
6 c 7 c

15.9 The Nightingale Effect

A

1 c 2 b 3 a

■ Add your marks for 15.7, 15.8 and 15.9 together to get a score out of 20 for reading comprehension.

B

There is a model reading of the text on the self-study cassette.

15.10 Franchising

B

The missing words are underlined:

1. an established product or service and a well-known brand image
2. an operating manual, showing how the business should be set up and how it must be run
3. help, advice and training in setting up the business
4. continuing advice, training and support during the life of franchise
5. the equipment that's required to set up and operate the business
6. stock of the product, which he will be able to obtain cheaply in bulk. This may result in savings or, depending on franchisor's mark-up, commit the franchisee to buying at above the market price.
7. local, national and even international advertising

C

Correct answers:

1 c 2 b 3 c 4 b 5 a
6 b 7 c 8 b 9 b 10 a

Acknowledgements

The authors and publishers are grateful to the authors, publishers and others who have given permission for the use of copyright material identified in the text. In cases where it has not been possible to identify the source of material used the publisher would welcome information from copyright owners.

Pages 10 and 11 British Telecom; page 117 Crossword Puzzle – David and Rosemary Brown; pages 123 and 124 City of Peterborough Development Corporation; page 126 Nightingale Secretariat.

Drawings by Clyde Pearson.
Artwork by Ace Art, Peter Ducker, Hard Lines, Reg Piggott and Wenham Arts.
Book designed by Peter Ducker MSTD.